To Julie from Dad & Mom
Christmas 1972

GINNY

GINNY

A True Story

by
MARY CARSON

DOUBLEDAY & COMPANY, INC., GARDEN CITY, NEW YORK

DEDICATION

This book is for

people who no longer believe in miracles,
to give them Faith;

people who face the impossible,
to show them Hope;

people who see only hardness or apathy
around them,
to teach them of Love;

and
to all who shared in this true story
and made it possible,
to express my Everlasting Gratitude.

CHAPTER 1

OCTOBER 25, 1966 WAS AN ORDINARY FALL DAY. IT WAS CLEAR AND A bit warmer than seasonable for the South Shore of Long Island. I was putting the finishing touches on a new school jumper for my six-year-old daughter, Ginny, and I really had no inkling whatever that this particular day would become etched deeply in my memory.

In fact, the only unusual feature of the moment was that the house was quiet. Seven of my eight children were in school. The youngest, seven-week-old Roberta, was sound asleep. The children were due home shortly and I was savoring the last few minutes of silence, thinking about the family—considering each one—wondering what the future held.

Dan and I had been married twelve years. We were both in our early thirties and the first seven of our eight children were born about a year apart. The three oldest were boys, the others all girls.

Paul, the oldest, was eleven. He was unusually tall, studious and maturing early. An avid reader, he did well in school, although his handwriting gave his teachers ulcers. He had a slow start as an infant, having had surgery to correct an intestinal blockage when he was just seven weeks old. As a very little boy, he had two hernia operations, but none of this seemed to affect his strength or energy now. He loved basketball, and his height gave him quite an advantage, but his usually peaceful nature prevented him from playing aggressively against smaller opponents.

Our second son was John. Ten-year-old John was never neutral. He plunged headlong into everything he did. He was either very good, or very bad. From the time he was a baby, I suspected he might become either an archbishop or an archcriminal.

Before he started school, he decided he wanted a typewriter. He spent days making one out of newspapers and toy building logs. The typing paper slipped between two logs, one of which turned, to help the paper advance. The trouble was that it didn't type like Daddy's—and he was heartbroken. John was continually trying to do things far beyond his ability; what he lacked in skill he overcompensated in endurance. It was often a frustrating task keeping his boundless enthusiasm channeled into constructive projects.

Joseph, the third boy, was nine, but because he was much shorter than his brothers, he seemed considerably younger than they. He had a sweet, trusting nature and a warm personality. His school-work was excellent, although he constantly confounded his teach-ers because he was always dreaming. They could never understand how he knew the answers when apparently he was not listening to the questions. He had a vivid imagination, which often led to fears. There was reportedly a great-uncle in the family who was quite a poet; possibly Joey inherited these traits from him.

Our oldest daughter was Theresa. Though she was sixteen months younger than Joe, and almost as tall, their personalities were similar and they were very close. One day Joey was out on a bike when a severe thunderstorm broke. She was genuinely con-cerned for his safety—keeping watch at the front door. As soon as she spotted him, she ran to me, her spirits restored. She met him at the back door, a big dry towel ready for him because she knew he would be drenched to the skin.

Although at times she could be quite an actress and was capable of keeping up a constant stream of little-girl chatter, she had a lot of good common sense. At eight she was most capable in the kitchen because she frequently helped me cook. That summer the heat had been intense. Being pregnant, I was often uncomfortable and exhausted. Theresa would frequently say, "You lie down and rest, Mommy. I'll do the dishes." . . . or the laundry or whatever needed to be done.

Bernadette was a natural "little mother." At seven, she had an awareness of others' problems, a virtue that some people never achieve in a lifetime. She had trouble with a muscle imbalance in her eyes that required an operation when she was in kindergarten.

She was so patient and good, even though it was quite painful. Almost a year later, it was decided that a second operation had to be performed. The doctor explained it to me; it was up to me to tell Dettie. Coming home from his office, I was mentally phrasing the best way to prepare her. She interrupted my thoughts. "Mommy, if I must have another operation, sometime, I don't mind."

At meals, when everyone was clamoring to be served first, she would say, "I don't mind if I'm last." Sometimes she would admonish the others, "Why don't we wait and let Mommy have something to eat?"

Bernadette frequently was quiet and thoughtful; at such times she was generally observing others and their needs. She was often criticized at school because she was nervous and unable to express herself in front of the class. She was shy, but possessed a goodness and sweetness that I would not have traded for the brashness and cockiness that gives some seven-year-olds self-confidence.

Virginia was six. Although a year younger, she and Dettie were inseparable. Being about the same height, they would often play "twins."

Ginny was the most industrious child I have ever known. She soon acquired the nickname, "the workin' kid" because she was always tidying up, changing beds and cleaning rooms. She was full of enthusiasm and spirit. But when she tired, she could go completely to pieces. If she had just finished cleaning the living room for a "present for Mommy" and one of the other children dumped toys, she would gladly have taken the culprit apart limb by limb— verbally, at least.

For a six-year-old, Ginny was a profound thinker, often delving into death and eternity. When Ginny was four my great-uncle, who lived nearby, died. She cried inconsolably. We were shocked at how broken up she was. Two days later, when Dan's father died, we dreaded breaking the news to Ginny because she was so close to Grandpa. When we did tell her she said, "That's good; now Grandpa and Uncle Charlie are together in heaven and they can keep each other company."

She had just started first grade at St. Christopher's with the older children and would often surprise her teacher with her ideas and questions. She had an assignment one day to bring in a picture of "something mighty that God had created." We searched magazines but, as it generally goes with such assignments, couldn't find pictures of anything appropriate. She suggested that she take a picture of all the children. As far as Ginny was concerned, our family was the greatest of God's works.

Ginny was open and candid. Though very young, she had a tremendous drive to take advantage of every minute, living life to its fullest.

Next was Celia. She would be five in a few months and had just started kindergarten. She was a warm, affectionate little child, with eyes that could melt marble. She loved everyone and could win anyone's heart. She had been the baby for a long time and thoroughly enjoyed it. Anytime she didn't feel like doing something, she would convince Ginny that she needed help.

There should be a fifty-fifty chance that shoes go on the right feet. One thing I couldn't understand was that Celia never got them to do so. We would devise all sorts of foolproof systems, yet they would invariably finish up wrong. The whole truth seemed to be that she honestly didn't care. There were too many things that needed to be done; flowers and bugs to watch, rain in the puddles, the sunset disappearing into clouds. There were ropes to jump, bikes to ride, trees that needed a little girl to climb. There was no time to be concerned about whether shoes were mated to the right feet.

Then there was little Roberta. She was sickly and not eating well, not gaining weight as she should. After my other deliveries, our family doctor, Frederick Metcalf of Rockville Centre, cheerfully told me how well the baby was doing, but with Roberta he looked troubled, and just asked me, "How does she look to you?"

I knew she wasn't as robust as the others, but I blamed it on a slightly premature birth. She was tiny and slept much of the time; her voice almost nonexistent. With a little extra care, I thought things would be fine. After all, Paul had outgrown his physical problems after a slow start.

She had difficulty eating those first few days and I told myself that it was just that the hospital schedule did not suit her. It would be fine when I took her home. At home, though, she slept more and ate less. I would wake her and work for hours, but could not coax her to eat. At three weeks she was still at her birth weight. Examination disclosed that she had a hole in her heart.

The big old house we lived in, so strangely quiet as these thoughts were passing through my mind, had belonged to my parents, and I had lived in it all my life. It is on Grand Avenue, the main street in Baldwin, Long Island. Its single disadvantage, the heavy traffic on the avenue, sometimes worried me, but Dan and I constantly cautioned the children about that danger and they seemed careful enough.

My mother and father, who lived just a few houses away, were the most loving grandparents any children could ever wish for.

Mom was often baking or working in her garden. The girls learned a great deal from her and, of course, there were usually bowls to lick, or apples to munch. Dad had a workshop in his cellar and a boat and was always willing to teach the boys all about both.

Just a few miles away in Freeport, Dan's mother lived in the house where Dan had grown up. Having had eight children of her own, she seemed, better than anyone, to understand life from a child's point of view. When she was with us, the children were all delighted. She would always listen to each of them—listen all the way through lengthy explanations of the latest exploit or accomplishment—and know just what the child wanted to hear from her.

Our family seemed to have average-type problems for average people. I had always felt that God never asks more of us than we can do. Somehow, the back and burden are made for each other. But we were very happy, and more than once Dan and I had spoken of the possibility that we were overdue for trouble. We had never had any really big problems.

Suddenly, the silence in the house was shattered. John burst in the back door—his eyes wide with terror, his face ashen.

"Ginny was hit by a truck!"

***

CHAPTER 2

He could barely manage the words to tell me where it had happened. Ginny had run out into the street—only a block and a half from home.

I told John to stay with the baby and ran . . . blindly. It was difficult to run. My legs ached—I was short of breath. Up ahead I could see a crowd. Almost as in a dream, it seemed that I was running hard, but getting no closer.

I prayed, "Dear God, please. . . ."

Many of the children, who were on their way home from school, knew me. I could hear voices: "It's Mrs. Carson, let her through." "That's Ginny's mother." The crowd separated.

Two little girls lay on the grass by the side of the road. In my heart, I wanted to gather Ginny into my arms. Something inside told me not to touch her; I could hurt her even more.

For a brief moment, I thought the other little girl was Bernadette. Then the second child cried and turned her head. "Thank God," my heart said, when I didn't recognize her. Thinking about it later, it seemed heartless that I should be relieved at what would become another's grief.

No one knew who the other child was, except that she was a classmate of Ginny's and they often walked home together. We went through her bookbag, but there was no identification. She was too frightened to be of any help.

It was hard to look at Ginny—yet I couldn't turn away. There were pools of blood on the street. The blood was running from her head. And, she was so still.

Joey was the first of my other children to come. He heard a policeman ask for a blanket. He took off his coat and covered his sister. One of her shoes had been thrown off. It was lying, crushed, by the side of the street. He picked up the shoe and her bookbag and said, "I'll take these home, Mommy." A nine-year-old can be purely gallant.

There were questions from the policeman and from other bystanders. I don't remember who they were or what they asked. There was one man, however, looking at Ginny, whom I could not forget. He came and asked if I was her mother. His face was filled with hopeless grief and compassion, so much deeper than the shock registered on the faces of the others that had gathered. I learned later that he was Dr. Stivelman. He lived right across the street from the scene of the accident. Hearing the commotion, he had come right out. Because of his knowledge, he recognized much that escaped me.

I heard the siren as the ambulance rounded the corner. In the past, I had always thought the sound of that siren alarming. Now it brought relief. They lifted Ginny to the stretcher—quickly, but gently. It was time to go.

The rest of my children had all gathered. I told them to go to "Aunt Alice." "Tell her what has happened. I'll call as soon as I can."

Alice was my next-door neighbor. She was so very close to me, she became Aunt Alice to my children. She had seven of her own, the eldest just a little older than mine.

She and her husband, Lee, were Ginny's godparents. One of life's greatest blessings is having a friend to whom you can send seven children, without warning, and know it will be all right.

In the ambulance, I asked the policeman, "Is she unconscious?" It was quite apparent that she was. My mind resisted asking, "Is she dead?" I was trying to convince myself that we were simply going to put a few stitches in the cut in her head and everything would be all right.

Once before, I had made a trip to the emergency room. Celia had fallen off the stoop and cut her head on a rock in the garden. It bled terribly. It was stitched and she came right home with me. But Celia had been running and crying—Ginny just lay there, motionless.

Ginny started to vomit. I felt I should try to clean it up. The policeman, a gentle, understanding man, put me at ease. "Don't you worry about the mess; it'll be cleaned up later. Just hang on to yourself. We'll be at the hospital in a minute."

Normally, in an accident, the patient is taken to the County Hospital, about eight miles away. I do not know who made the decision to take her to South Nassau Communities Hospital which was less than a mile away, but I am grateful to whoever it was. Both hospitals are excellent, but I realize now there probably would not have been time to drive the extra distance.

We spent most of the trip trying to get the other little girl to tell us her name and address—to little avail. We turned sharply around corners. It was an effort to keep the girls from sliding off the stretchers.

All the turns confused me. I knew the route well; I hadn't been watching the roads. For a second, when we arrived, I wondered if we were at South Nassau after all. Then I realized since I had last been there, the emergency room had been moved to a new wing on the opposite side of the building.

The driver and policeman ran inside with Ginny. I stayed in the ambulance with the other little girl. My heart was tearing me away, but I knew it wouldn't be safe to leave her alone for a few minutes, and she needed someone to console her—probably more than I did at the moment. When they came back and took her into the emergency room, I followed them.

I don't know how many people were working on Ginny. They were ripping off her dress and someone was suctioning out her mouth. There was great speed but an air of competency, not confusion.

An aide ushered me out before I had taken two steps into the room. She was not annoyed that I had gone where I did not belong. She said simply, "I'll need a little information. Will you come with me?"

We went to her office and she took the usual statistics. I was surprised that I knew Ginny's birth date right off. I can give all the children's birthdays in order, but to pick one out of the middle requires a cool head. As she took down the information, the clerk marveled that I was so calm.

The necessary forms were all filled out. I asked if I could call Dan and let him know what had happened. There was some difficulty getting an outside line. The police and emergency staff had all the phones tied up. Finally, a line was open that I could have for a few minutes. I went to the phone and realized suddenly how worried I really was. I couldn't remember Dan's office number. I dialed automatically—hoping I was correct.

At that point, I had no positive report on Ginny's condition. I did not want to overwhelm him, and I still clung steadfastly to the deep hope that things were not as grave as they seemed. I decided that it was better to try not to alarm him, and fill in more of the details after he reached the hospital.

I told him Ginny had been in an accident and I did not know how serious it was. They were working on her in the emergency room. I would appreciate it if he could get away from work and come over to stay with me until we knew where we stood.

Some time later he told me that I had been so calm on the phone that he had no inkling of how serious the situation was. I was pleased. I am not much of an actress and was glad I had not conveyed any fear. I did not want him worrying while he was driving.

Then I began to walk—back and forth—afraid to walk out of sight of the emergency-room door. I was sure that, at any moment, someone would come through that door with reassuring words about Ginny. I couldn't risk not being right there. I paced the length of the hall innumerable times—watching, waiting. The clerk suggested that I sit in the waiting room, but it was easier to keep walking. I felt so helpless. I would have been willing to do anything to help, but there was nothing I could do but wait . . . and pray. Since it was impossible to concentrate, the only thing I could ask was "Dear God—please."

Frequently, the door to the emergency room would open. Each time I held my breath, hoping it was someone looking for me. A nurse would run across the hall to a supply room, grab something, run back—and the door would close again. I tried to observe what equipment they carried, possibly to guess what was happening. Having no nursing experience, I could determine nothing but extreme gravity and great haste.

＊

CHAPTER 3

DAN'S OFFICE WAS IN THE NEXT TOWN. IT WAS ONLY MINUTES TILL HE arrived—but it seemed like hours. With him there, it was easier. He is always strong and calm—a sure support when I am in need.

We walked together. Our voices were low, the words measured before spoken. Each was trying to strengthen the other. There was little I could tell him. I related what I knew of the accident. He had spent many months as a soldier in combat in Korea and seemed, better than I, to grasp from my description the severity of her injuries.

Everyone was frantically busy, every second urgent; I didn't want to stop anyone to ask for information. And so, we walked together, and thought, and wondered . . . and prayed.

The outside door opened. One of our parish priests came in. He nodded to us, but rushed right into the emergency room. It was then that I gave up hope that they were just going to "put in a few stitches" and send her home. They don't call a priest unless things are critical. It was hard to admit it to myself. I just held Dan's hand more tightly and said nothing.

Within a few minutes, Father came back and spoke to us. He gave us no medical report. They had called him to come right over for the "last rites." Now I understood the reason behind the proposal to change the name of this ritual to "sacrament of the sick." The priest read the shock in my face when he referred to it as the last rites, and he spent some minutes explaining to us.

Frequently, he said, the special prayers saved for such a crucial moment have wondrous effects and restore bodily health. However, he did mention that a child of such tender age could not be guilty of any sin and was certainly assured a place in heaven.

I thought to myself that it was somewhat incongruous for him to be mentioning the "restoration of bodily health" and "a place in heaven" all in one breath. He had just seen her. Was she already gone—and was he preparing the way for a doctor to break the news to us? But I knew him to be too honest and direct a man to mislead us. If she were dead, he would have told us. Therefore, she must still be alive—there *was* hope.

Father left, and again . . . we walked. I tried to say a Rosary but could not keep my mind on it. I kept going back to "Dear God, please. . . ."

Finally a doctor came out of the emergency room. He introduced himself as, "Dr. Burstein, a neurosurgeon" and told us that he just happened to be in the hospital when Ginny was brought in. I felt my prayers were already being answered.

I guess I pictured all neurosurgeons as looking like Vince Edwards of TV's "Ben Casey." Dr. Burstein didn't look the part. He was really a very ordinary-looking man, but his manner conveyed the impression of extraordinary competence to me. I immediately felt confidence in him, as he described Ginny's injuries.

She had severely depressed fractures of both sides of her skull. Her eyes were no longer responding to light. (I learned later that the contact between the optic nerve and the brain is one of the last functions to stop before death.) He suspected there were clots in her brain. If he did not operate, there was practically no chance she would live. If he did, he would give her one-in-a-million to make it through the night. Because it was a child, he felt he wanted to try for that one chance. He would shave her head, drill holes and probe, looking for clots. Could he have our permission? Time was of the utmost importance. (Though it seemed much longer, it had been only about an hour since the accident.) Because of brain damage caused by lack of oxygen, he would have to operate immediately. We agreed he should do whatever he could to save her.

Again, we walked—and each thought his own private thoughts. Some months later we talked about that afternoon and it was surprising how similar those thoughts had been. We both had had the same reaction . . . a million-to-one are brutal odds. Would she make it? Each of us had wondered if we were being unreasonable, subjecting her to all she would have to undergo? If she lived, she could be left completely incapacitated—or in any stage between that and normalcy. If she died, how do you wake a child? Only a few weeks before, we had mentioned the possibility of buying a cemetery plot—and cast off the idea because its need was too remote. I had never been to a child's funeral. How difficult would it be? If they shaved her head, the casket would have to be closed. Dan had wondered if that was why Dr. Burstein had so clearly emphasized the fact that he would have to shave her head? I still had the dress I wore at my first communion. Would the veil cover her head so that the casket could be open?

The thoughts started to become overwhelming and I deliberately stopped myself. "Dear God—please—don't take her. She's got to get better."

If I were to pray for her with any sincerity, I had to pray that she would recover completely! I certainly was not going to pray that she would recover only partially. I am not one for making bargains with God. I promised nothing in return. Promises made under such an emotional strain are often unreasonable, and easily broken. No promise at all seemed more honest—and I had to be completely honest with God. He knew me too well. All I could offer Him was the complete sincerity of a pierced heart. God certainly *could* make her better—I had to believe that He *would!* He gave me that Faith to believe that He would!

We were asked to go to the pediatrics ward. They needed Ginny's medical history; any allergies or current medications. Hope surged in me at the request. If they wanted her history, it meant they still believed she had a chance. It was only a straw, but I clung fiercely to it. "Dear God," I prayed, as the nurse entered our answers to each question.

They asked if we wanted to wait down in the lobby. Because of the other children, we felt it better that we go home. The doctor would call when the operation was over. We would come back then.

We tried to retrace our steps to the emergency entrance, but were confused. A nurse in the elevator gave us directions. (Several days later she came to visit me. She lived right across the street from us. I had never known her because the busy road is a barrier to friendship. Now, since the accident, the traffic seemed heavier than ever. She had come over simply because she had heard about our little girl. It wasn't till she came to the door that we both realized we had been together that afternoon in the elevator—and she had helped us in our confusion.)

Driving home, we passed the scene of the accident, now barricaded by the police. The road showed fresh chalk marks, indicating exact locations; a precaution taken if a fatality is expected.

A large moving van was parked by the side of the road. It seemed so huge; Ginny so small . . . I shuddered.

I tried to plan how to tell the children. It was good to have every one of them. For their sake, I had to hold on—no tears—no big scene. They, too, had to believe that God would give her back to us!

It is stabilizing to learn how much grief your heart can contain without spilling over to the outside!

When we arrived at Alice's I told her what little we actually knew. The change in her appearance was startling. Alice is tiny, but she has handsome features showing determined self-confidence. Our report showed its effect. Her resolute bearing was suddenly frail, stricken. She closed her eyes for a second. The love between us was deep and I could feel her heart breaking with mine. I did not want to hurt her, yet the truth was harsh.

The children all gathered and, as simply as I could, I told them that Ginny was hurt badly, very badly. We had to pray so hard. As wild and silly as that many kids can be at times, when you really need them, they come through.

Alice would have kept us all for supper, but I was anxious to be home, alone with the children, for a while. As always, she understood.

We made the necessary phone calls to Dan's mother and mine—then waited for the doctor to call.

My father was not yet home from work. As hard as it would be for me to tell him, I did not want him to hear it from anyone else. I watched my parents' house from my kitchen window till his cab pulled up, then went right over. I walked with him into his house. Once more, I tried to be simple and matter-of-fact. He took me in his arms and I had to struggle desperately to keep from sobbing. Being the only girl in the family, I had always been very close to Dad. It was heartbreaking for him. Thinking about it later, I realized I had one child hurt; Dad had two. My brother Joe had just lost his wife, Nancy, to cancer; now I could lose Ginny. For me it was one child, but Dad had both a son and a daughter who had been dealt severe blows. But he is wise and strong and, instead of breaking under the strain of his own feelings, he reinforced my courage and sent me back home to fix dinner.

The children were all solemn and quietly ate their meal. I tried, but the first mouthful stuck in my throat like dry cotton. Dan made an attempt, but he did no better.

Dad and Dan's mother came over and it was good to have them to talk to. My mother was taking care of Joe's children. We assured her that we would call her as soon as there was any word. It was hard to keep any conversation going. When the phone rang, I held my breath as Dan answered it. Each time it was someone asking for word, offering to help in any way they could.

At last, Dr. Burstein called. Ginny was still alive! It was now three and a half hours that she had survived!

"Thank you, God. Please keep helping her."

Unfortunately, the doctor's report was not "everything is going to be all right." He had opened her skull but found no clots. He had elevated the depressed bones, cleaned out all the chips. But, he admitted honestly that he did not really know if he had helped her. Her brain was badly bruised. He could not change her chances —one-in-a-million—that she would live through the night! I leaned heavily on the word "bruised." He had not said "damaged." It seemed to me that bruised cells would heal; damaged or destroyed cells could not.

Dad said he would answer any phone calls. Dan's mother took care of the children, leaving us free to go right over.

I can still feel the effort that it took to walk from the car to the hospital. I was compelled by a force of responsibility that hurt all over. Blinded to all but the straight course to our destination, I seemed to feel that any distraction would slow my progress and that somehow my being with her was suddenly going to cure everything.

But then we entered the room and it was suddenly obvious that it was not a nightmare. All the reports were true. The only thing that made it any easier was that if I had had to identify her, I could not have done it. Her head was so swollen and battered, it did not look like that sunny, angelic face that had called "Good-by" that morning, running off to school.

The array of equipment was unbelievable! I would have stood and kept watch—eating my heart out. Dan knew better, put his arm around my shoulder and led me out of the room. "We really can't do anything to help her by staying here. She is unconscious and doesn't know if we are here or not. We'll only be in the way. The other children need us more."

At that time, I did not know that Dan was carrying one extra burden in his heart. He had one other message from the doctor that he hadn't told me. The doctor had said to him, "If you want to see your daughter *alive* once more, you better get to the hospital immediately." I left the room, expecting to come back in the morning; Dan didn't.

Sometimes, now, I feel bad that he carried all that weight alone. But, maybe it was better. I still believed in that one chance.

The nurses said "if anything happens" they would call. Why is it more delicate to say "if anything happens" than to say "if she dies," when we all clearly understood what was implied? Maybe it is that "if anything happens" does leave open the remote alternative that she might wake up and call for us, although I'm afraid I was the only one who even slightly considered that possibility.

We went in to see the other little girl who was injured with Ginny. She was a beautiful little child; her long curly brown hair hung in limp, damp waves. The strain of the day showed as fright on her face. We finally learned that her name was Jeanne Berry. Her folks had moved here only recently. They had ten children but Jeanne was the only one in St. Christopher's school. She and Ginny used to walk home together. She had no real memory of the accident itself, although she did remember my being in the ambulance with her.

She had a broken leg and collarbone and was being tested for internal injuries. It seemed that everything would be fine.

Her outlook was saintly. She was not upset by her own discomfort, but was concerned for Ginny's welfare. She wanted to see Gin but the nurses agreed that Ginny's appearance would only upset her. Since Jeanne was in traction and couldn't be moved, she accepted this as a reason though she couldn't understand it.

Jeanne was a remarkable little girl. She never complained for herself—and promised to pray for Ginny.

We came back home and finally had a chance to sit down and talk with John. He had been right across the street when the accident happened. The girls had run out into the street. He heard the screech of brakes, saw his sister's limp body sliding along the pavement. He kept saying, over and over, "I thought she would never stop! She just kept sliding on the street!" He had run to her and recognized that she was hurt badly. As long as some adults had gathered, they would take care of Ginny. The best thing he could do was to run and get me.

He was upset and it was difficult for him to talk about it. John and Ginny were four years apart and frequently unhappy with each other. Suddenly he loved her desperately. He kept asking, "Why did she run out?" We wondered the same thing.

The normal pattern after dismissal from school spread the children out over more than a half mile. Some had already passed; some were nearby, others still further down the road. There were many versions of what had happened. Someone said that she had run across to her grandmother. My mother was ten miles away with my brother's children; Dan's mother was at work in the next town.

There was a smashed pumpkin in the street. One story told that she was on her way home from purchasing a pumpkin for Halloween. Another involved a lunch box. Ginny didn't carry a lunch box.

The only thing that could be positively established was that a gardener's truck was parked by the side of the road. Ginny, followed by Jeanne, had run out in front of the parked truck, into the path of the moving vehicle.

But, no one could answer the question "*Why* had she run out?" Ginny was an alert, sensible little girl. She honestly knew better. More mysterious was why Jeanne had followed her. Ginny was on the wrong side of Grand Avenue; Jeanne was not. Besides, Jeanne was only half a block from the corner at which she turned. The only reason imaginable was the possibility that something had frightened both of them. Had something caused them to panic? It may never be explained.

We had been asked by our attorneys not to talk to the truck driver. It was obvious there would be a legal action as a result of the accident. It would have been inadvisable for us to communicate with him. Yet, I wanted to. For all the grief in my heart, I could only imagine the agony in his. We had learned he had young children of his own. He would not deliberately do something like this. I hoped that he didn't hate Ginny.

His wife must have been caught in the same turmoil, and not warned of the legal entanglements . . . she called me. When she introduced herself, I did not recognize her name. With remarkable courage, she explained, "It was my husband that was driving the truck."

With deep concern, I asked her, "How is he?" She said he was terribly shaken and upset, and from her voice it was obvious that she too was suffering. She wanted me to know that he had done everything he could to avoid it, but she had run so close to the truck that he couldn't stop in time. He hadn't done it intentionally. It was so painful for her to put it into words.

I tried to assure her that we felt no ill will toward him. The most important thing for him was to know that it was an accident, and to get hold of himself and go back to work . . . for his own sake, for her and for their children.

She promised me their prayers for Ginny's recovery.

I told Dan about the call, and meant it with all my heart, when I said to him, "As difficult as this is for us, I wouldn't trade places with him for anything in the world!"

I called Dr. Metcalf. He had taken care of all of us for over twenty years. He was a kind, fatherly man, who completely fitted the image of the dedicated "family doctor." Sometimes, people speak of general practitioners with some disdain. They feel you must see a specialist for everything. But I could never agree with them. I always had complete confidence in Dr. Metcalf. He would take care of anything that he could. But when he felt that something was more than he should handle, he would immediately recommend a specialist. Knowing this, I trusted him completely.

Four weeks before Ginny's accident I had taken Roberta to Dr. Metcalf for a routine check up. After he examined her, I was waiting for him, listening to the music on the radio. A full chorus started, "*When you walk through a storm, keep your head up high. . . .*" It struck me as most appropriate background music if someone was sick, but I was here, full of joy with my three-week-old angel.

He sat down, folded his hands on his desk, and started on the end of a sigh. (I had gotten to know him well. That sigh was the beginning of something he would rather not have to tell you.) "Well, Mary, she has had a heart murmur since birth. It should have stopped by now. It may still clear up by itself, but I would feel better if you take her to a pediatric cardiologist." The chorus was finishing, *"Walk on, walk on, with hope in your heart. . . ."*

While that music gave me some courage then, I had no idea how often I would think of that incident in the next few weeks.

In filling out the emergency-room forms, they had asked the name of my doctor. When they had called Dr. Metcalf he had given instructions that each phase of her needs be assigned to the best specialist available.

Now, almost six hours after the accident, this phone call was the first opportunity I had to talk to him. It must have been difficult for him to counsel me. He had always particularly liked Ginny . . . and she liked him. (I could still see him holding her and playing with her as a little infant.)

He started with that same sigh, "Well, Mary, I wish there was something else I could tell you. She's a very sick little girl. We'll just have to keep hoping. I'll look in on her; there will be specialists for everything. But I want you to know that at South Nassau, with the doctors that are working on her, she is getting the best care possible—anywhere. Everything that can be, will be done for her."

I thanked him and was grateful. I had such confidence in him that it removed any doubts about the possibility of more chance somewhere else. I knew if "anything happened" it would not be for inadequate medical care.

Whenever I would waver, I would remind myself that God has the last word. She could go right to the last breath, and He could still bring her back.

"Dear God, please. . . ."

It was difficult getting the children settled down to sleep. Each of them offered special night prayers for Ginny, but many of them were sobbing softly as they did. Celia shared a room with Ginny. When I went to tuck her in, the empty bed bothered both of us. I took her hand, and she came down the hall and doubled up with Theresa and Bernadette. It was easier for me to avoid that room completely, and better for Celia to be with the other two girls.

Dan's mother had fed the baby. My father had helped the children tidy up and do the dishes. One of Dan's brothers and several of the neighbors came. It must have been difficult for them to come, but it was so good to have them with us. The faith, love and composure that everyone radiated were unforgettable.

The phone rang constantly. Still fearing a call from the hospital, I held my breath each time it rang . . . and prayed again.

Dan would answer. All conversation would stop. It was always similar, "She's still alive . . . there is no way of knowing yet . . . if she makes it through the night, it's a good sign . . . she's in a coma . . . no, we don't know if there are any other injuries; everything depends upon her head."

It continued all evening. Many apologized for calling, for "disturbing" us; but their calls gave us encouragement. Each promised to pray—to have Masses said—to have their children and the children's schools all pray. The doorbell rang; a telegram was delivered. It read, "Our prayers are with you, R. H. J. H." The initials belonged to the Very Reverend Msgr. Richard H. J. Hanley, editor of our diocesan newspaper . . . and a friend. Before long it amounted to literally millions of prayers that were being offered.

Around ten, there was another call. Dan answered, but something had changed. Everyone listened intently. There were cautious glances toward me, which I could not return. I stared at the floor and prayed more desperately than ever. Instead of his usual conversation, it was simply, "Yes . . . oh . . . no . . . all right." It was so different from the previous calls that I was positive it was the hospital. Everyone felt the same apprehension. He finished and came back into the living room. I looked up at him, steeling myself for the report.

Having been in on both sides of the call, he hadn't realized how it had sounded to all of us. It was his sister. She was a nurse at another of the local hospitals, but several of her friends worked at South Nassau. She had just been talking to one who knew about Ginny. There was no new information; just a confirmation of the opinions that the doctors had expressed. Things looked very bad.

The relief that it hadn't been the hospital brought a mixture of laughter and tears. She was still alive. She still had a chance.

It was getting late. Everyone had to get up for work in the morning. They all left, asking us to let them know if we heard anything.

For the first time since the afternoon, we were alone. We were both exhausted, but couldn't sleep. Everything had been said. Restless, Dan turned on the television. He was looking at it, but not seeing or hearing. His whole consciousness was locked deep within his heart.

You hurt so much and there is absolutely nothing you can do to help or hurry anything.

When I am worried or upset, I find my mind much easier to control if my hands are busy. There was a full basket of ironing to be done, so I worked on it till two in the morning.

There is a great therapy in work. When you have a consuming grief in your heart, it is easier if you don't try to sleep until you are too exhausted to think. As soon as you slacken your deliberate control, your grief escapes your heart into your mind and soon spills over to the outside and to others. In such a great crisis, other hearts are already filled with their own tears. They do not need yours to add to theirs. So, you can try to keep it deep inside and not hurt anyone else.

We listened all night. Thank God, the phone never rang!

✻✻✻

CHAPTER 4

SEVEN THE NEXT MORNING, WE CALLED THE HOSPITAL. PATIENT INFOR-
mation is generally given from one central desk. Because of the
critical circumstances, they connected us with the pediatric ward.
From the phone, the nurse could see directly into her room. "She
made it through the night, and is still holding on. Come whenever
you want. You're not restricted to visiting hours."

Children are wonderful. The brightest part of any tragedy is an
excuse to stay home from school. Thinking it over, we decided it
was best for all of us to keep going, as much as possible, with our
regular responsibilities. Dan took them to school, a little late, to
avoid any preclass conversation.

The Sisters at St. Christopher's were deeply concerned and most
understanding.

The phrase "Sister says" holds marvelous power, and I wonder if
the saints in heaven quake as much as school children at its impli-
cations. If Sister says, "Make Ginny well," do the saints dare ask
God for anything less? The Sisters and teachers, the school children,
the parishioners at daily Mass, everyone prayed.

Alice came over to take care of Roberta and Celia, and Dan and
I left for the hospital. The staff at pediatrics were the most compas-
sionate professionals I had ever met!

Ginny had been moved. She was now in a private room, separated
from the nurses' desk by a glass wall. She was watched constantly.

We went in and I took her hand. It was so cold. Because her
tongue had swollen and completely filled her mouth, they had done
a tracheotomy in the emergency room. She was breathing hard
through the opening in her throat. Oxygen was connected directly

to the trachea opening. A complete assortment of intensive-care equipment was all in operation—a drain in her nose, a catheter and intravenous tubes.

Her bed was covered with an "ice blanket"—a double layer of plastic, sealed in such a way as to make a continuous pattern of tubes. A mechanical unit connected to it circulates a refrigerant through the tubes, back to the "ice box" which keeps it at the desired temperature. When the body temperature is kept low, the brain requires less oxygen. Even at the risk of pneumonia, they had to keep her cool. Any clothing would warm her body, so it was avoided. The ice blanket was covered with a cotton sheet blanket; her only covering was an infant's receiving blanket.

There was a nurse with Ginny at all times, watching all the apparatus, constantly checking vital signs. Her blood pressure was taken so frequently they didn't even bother to remove the band from her arm.

Her little body lay still. With the helmet of bandages, her head seemed enormous. Her face was swollen. Her left eye was black from her eyebrow to the middle of her cheek. Her eyes were closed, the lids showing only a trace of movement. The right side of her face was scraped raw from her forehead almost to her mouth. Her knuckles and wrists were scraped to the bone. There was blood in the catheter bag; she was bleeding internally.

Doctors checked her constantly. Some were the doctors who were taking care of her, but others had heard about her and had come to see for themselves. They came just to see this "living miracle." With each doctor, we'd look for some encouragement—some positive outlook on the possibility of her recovery. It was always, "We'll just have to wait and see."

It is difficult to visit an unconscious child. There is nothing you can do; it eats your heart out just to stand and watch. The nurses' care of her was complete and competent, so intricate that I was afraid to get involved. She had less ability than a newborn infant. She could not open her eyes, breathe or move without help. She could not even control her own body temperature.

I felt helpless. I would stand by her bed, hold her hand . . . and pray.

We went down the hall to visit Jeanne. When she woke up that morning, she didn't know how she got into the hospital, nor did she remember my being in the ambulance with her. Her mother had been talking to her, trying to learn more about the accident. Jeanne wanted to help, and was trying, but it was obvious that the shock had erased all details. It had been our best chance of learning the answer to "Why had they run out?" Now the reason was blotted from her memory—or possibly there was no reason. Maybe it was better that we did not know.

Again, it was good for us to keep busy, so we went home. It was good that with eight children there was interminable washing and ironing. Time passed more quickly when I kept busy and it was easier knowing there was work that had to be done.

The neighbors would come, take care of the baby, help with much of the work—and just talk. It is easier to face a problem when you can talk about it—and it's much easier to have courage if you are not alone.

Many of our neighbors I've known since childhood. I grew up with the daughter of a woman who still lived a few houses away. She was fond of my children and often stopped to talk. We had a common interest in gardening, and she frequently supplied me with plants that she could grow faster than I could starve them. The children often ran down to visit her. Just a few weeks before, she had taken Ginny and Bernadette to the beach with her granddaughters.

She came to the door. Heaven only knows what it took out of her to come. Her face showed control and sympathy . . . and a deep compassion. (She had lost a son when he was Ginny's age.) She had heard that Ginny was killed. It broke her heart, but she had to come and be with me.

Even though we honestly did not know if Ginny would live, she was relieved and thankful that she had some chance. What had started as a visit to comfort the bereaved, finished as an opportunity to reinforce the hope of the afflicted.

We received a phone call from a couple in the next town. They had heard about Ginny and just wanted to try to give us a little hope. Six months before, their three-year-old son had been hit by a car. His injuries had been similar, his chances of recovering about the same. The same doctors had operated. In fact, he had been in the same room as Ginny. He was getting better.

They didn't want to intrude, but hoped it would help if we knew their son had lived through it. It was the nearest thing to a ray of hope anyone had offered us. They told us to feel free to call them anytime we wanted. While the boy's recovery did not guarantee anything for Ginny, still it helped so much to have their experience to lean on.

Afternoon and evening we returned to the hospital. Each time there was disappointment when we entered the room and found no improvement in Ginny's condition. I would resign myself to the fact that there was no startling recovery, and begin to search for minute improvements—any little recognizable sign of improvement.

But, there was nothing. Always she lay so still, so cold. Her breathing was fast and hard. She seemed to be fighting so desperately to live . . . but she had so little to fight with.

Again, we listened for the phone all night . . . again it never rang. At seven the next morning, we checked with the hospital. She had lived through a second night!

As soon as we were free to leave, we went back to visit her again. Now my hopes were higher than ever. They had felt that she couldn't live through the first night. She had made it through the second! Surely, there was going to be some sign this morning. Bypassing the elevator, we ran up the stairs and hurried to her room.

Nothing had changed. The doctors were still reserved, afraid to let us hope. All they could tell us was that there could be no way of knowing; we would just have to wait and see.

We met Dr. Metcalf in the hall. I had hoped that, knowing him better, he might give us information which the specialists did not feel free to impart. There still was nothing to tell us. With a great compassion, he said, "Take care of yourselves." As he started to leave, he turned to me and advised, "Just keep your chin up."

We returned home, had a little lunch and I tried to get things done before the children came home from school. Ginny was on my mind constantly. It was almost forty-eight hours since the accident. She had lived this long, and she was working so hard, she had to get better.

The phone rang. It was the hospital! How intensely and desperately you can pray in the split second between "this is pediatriacs" and the first sentence. Ginny's lung had collapsed. They would have to drain an air pocket in her chest. Could they have our permission?

Dan was working in his office at home. While I was relaying the message, I was trying to convince myself that, while it did not sound good, at least she was still alive.

We went right over. The drive seemed long, the walk from the car to the entrance even longer. The stairs seemed steep, each step stabbing pain deep in my chest.

By the time we got there, the air was drained, the lung inflated. They watched intently.

The lung was holding!

The day before, Ginny had been breathing hard. Innocently, I had looked on it as a sign of her fight to live—a strength amid so much weakness. In reality, she was working desperately against a chest filling with air.

Now that the chest was drained, she was breathing smoothly. No longer was there that shallow gasping. Finally we got some medical encouragement. Dr. Gelfand, the chest specialist, felt that as long as the lung held, she had a chance to live! Instead of offering that standard, "We'll just have to wait and see," he smiled down at her and said, "I think she's going to make it." He was the first doctor who was the least bit optimistic.

"Dear God, thank you!"

We went home. Now we had renewal of our hope . . . and even firmer foundation for our faith. The great joy began to work on my strained nerves. Since the moment of the accident, I had kept everything in tight rein. All the emotion that I had been holding down, burst forth. I went up to our room, closed the door, lay down and cried.

Dan came up and we sat and talked for a long time. It had gotten to him the night before. I had been able to reassure him. Now he was comforting me. We recognized that if we could stagger our "lows," we could help each other and, somehow, we would get through.

***

CHAPTER 5

THE ENDLESS, LOVING CARE THE NURSES GAVE GINNY WAS A BEAUTIFUL expression of devotion. The constant turning and massage to maintain her skin; the patience to do the same jobs over and over—and over again; all conveyed their affection. Considering the damage to her brain, she had no right to be alive. But now that she had a chance to live, their enthusiasm soared. Each one seemed to take a deep personal interest, almost as if it were her own child lying in that bed. They all talked to her as they were working on her, explaining each movement, as if she could understand. "I'm going to take your blood pressure, now. Can you feel it on your arm?" "I have to give you a shot, but it will be over in a second."

They explained to us that the first faculty to return is hearing. Whenever we were there, we were to try to talk to her. At some point she would hear, and it would be good for her to hear our voices.

We'd talk, but it was so difficult. What do you say to such a lifeless little body?

Each time we came, we'd tell her that she had been hit by a truck, and was badly hurt. We kept repeating the same explanation, not knowing when she would hear or understand. We felt that when she woke up, she had to know what had happened and where she was. We told her she was in the same hospital where she had had her tonsils taken out. The doctors and nurses were all working with her, helping her get better. Everything was going to be all right.

Then what do you say? . . .

By the third morning, Dan's office work was piling up and he just could not take time to visit Ginny during the day. It was quite an emotional strain to visit her, and he felt it would be better if I did not go alone. Alice was free, so we went together. I knew what to expect, but was afraid that it would be hard on her. She had been a nurse, and I was sure that she had seen patients in such a condition, but it is different when it touches someone so close to you.

I tried to prepare her, but she assured me that she knew, and it would be all right.

We went into the room. Alice was standing at the foot of her bed. Ginny was motionless as I took her hand and called softly, "Hi, Ginny. It's Mommy." Alice saw her foot move!

You pray it's hearing and understanding, but wonder if it's only a muscle spasm.

We were so elated, but the professionals smiled patiently and just said, "It could be, but it's a little soon to be sure."

The doctors were amazed that she had made it so far, but not one of them was willing to make any prediction. One doctor finally said that they had done what they could medically. Now, it was between Ginny and God!

That afternoon, Sister Agnes, Ginny's first-grade teacher, and Sister St. James, the principal, came to the hospital. Besides Ginny and Jeanne, there was a third little girl from the same class who was being tested for a possible brain tumor. It must have been most difficult for them.

When we were children, we really never knew the Sisters. We were taught that they were apart from the world, and we thought they were unaffected by it. We never considered that they had families or friends, likes or dislikes, loves and fears. Fortunately, that "image" is disappearing.

That afternoon, more than ever before, I realized how deeply human they are. (That is not meant as a criticism—Christ was fully human, too.) Their hearts, just as a mother's, can fill with tears—and break.

Sister Agnes came in and talked to Ginny, but her eyes were misty, her voice unsteady. She told of the other children in the class, how they were all asking for her. Every day they prayed she would be back soon.

Sister Agnes was a very young and buoyant personality. Sister St. James, though young in spirit, had a few more years' experience.

Seeing Ginny must have affected her deeply. That battered little body looked pitiful and hopeless. She came to the door of Ginny's room, but could not come in. I admired her courage in coming.

The days wore on. We visited two or three times a day. The intravenous needle was moved from her arm to her leg and back again. She was losing weight, and starting to bruise from all the needle holes. They tried to feed her a little milk through a tube in her nose. For some reason, this was the only treatment I found repulsive. There was something about pouring milk in a child's nose that made me gag.

It became apparent that she would be in a state of coma for some time and the decision was made to do a gastrostomy, inserting a feeding tube directly through the abdominal wall into the stomach. Dr. Noto, a pediatric surgeon, was called to do the procedure. With the tube in her stomach, they were able to remove the nasal drain. She looked substantially better with her nose clear.

They started feeding her "instant breakfast" every hour, an ounce at a time. Gradually it was increased in quantity, until her intake of fluid was sufficient; the intravenous could be stopped. Every time some apparatus left that room, we had made another stride!

Evidently the kitchen did not know that all that "instant breakfast" was not being taken orally. They must have kept records, because the flavors were carefully rotated so that she would not get tired of one kind. As with everything else, the nurses would talk to Ginny about it. "You have strawberry for lunch today. Do you like that better than the chocolate you had for breakfast?"

The lung was fine and she no longer received the oxygen. The tracheotomy showed a metal plate with a small hole in the center, on her throat. A curved metal tube, about two and a half inches long, was inserted through the hole, down into her windpipe. As the tube constantly filled with mucus, she was regularly suctioned. A flexible, plastic tube was passed into her windpipe, through the metal tube, and a machine drew the mucus away, relieving her breathing. Whenever they did it, it would gag her. In rebellion, she would wince and pull her arms and legs. Another sign of life!

It was difficult to talk constantly, so I read to her by the hour. I had a collection of children's poetry, a book given to me by my father when I was Ginny's age. The pages were yellow and brittle; the covers had broken off, and I had taped them back on, but accidentally got them on upside down.

I was sitting by the side of her bed, completely absorbed, because I thoroughly enjoyed children's poetry. I glanced up and noticed a nurse standing at the door, staring at the book. She knew it had been a grueling time for me, but could not figure out why I was reading with the book upside down.

Gin seemed to have periods when she was restless and other times when she was peaceful, comparable to a conscious person's being awake or asleep. When reading to her, I would wonder if I was tiring her—if she might prefer that I stop so she could rest. I would pause and ask her, "Ginny, if you want me to keep reading, move your leg." Sometimes it would move.

When she did not respond, I did not know if she was unable to move—or deliberately did not move so that I would stop.

She was soon able to move her limbs on command (not always the one I requested—but some movement) often enough, that I was sure she was hearing and understanding.

I would try to prove it to the doctors or the nurses. She seemed to try so hard, but was unable to control anything the way she wanted. Skeptical, they explained that it could be just a muscle contracting involuntarily.

You can't make medical proof out of things a mother feels in her heart.

Sister Agnes visited faithfully every week. She brought "get well" cards which the children had made in class for Ginny. I would read them to her and began to wonder if several of the boys in the class were named "Timmy." Finally I caught on. "Timmy" was the new word they had just learned and many of them included it—possibly to keep her in touch with their academic progress.

I began to notice that she definitely was responding more to some of the cards. When I would tell her who had made the card, sometimes there was movement in her arms or legs. I separated them and the next time Sister came, I showed her the ones that seemed to stir something within Ginny. She looked through the stack and had an expression of that same belief that I could feel. The chosen cards were from the children who sat nearest her in school!

Her right eye, having the lesser injury, had begun to open a few days after the accident, but it would roll uncontrollably to the corner. When she started to be able to hold it in a fixed position, it would stare blankly. But now there were times when we felt, positively, that she was seeing!

The left eye was still swollen, but the black and purple were being replaced by green and yellow around the edges of the bruise.

We saw steady, though slow, improvement and had adjusted to her over-all appearance. We started bringing other members of the family. The first visit was always difficult. We had been talking about her "getting better," but to someone seeing her for the first time, it was a heartbreaking experience. But they are a remarkably courageous group and would come with us again. Each one was heartened by the second visit. She really was getting better. You just needed something worse with which to compare it.

In her coma, Ginny began to tighten all the tendons in her arms and legs. Her arms pulled up against her chest; her hands clenched into fists, turned toward the inside of her wrists. Her knees pulled up; her feet extended, and her toes pointed down in what was known as "foot drop."

Wooden blocks were brought, covered with blankets and braced at the foot of her bed. Each time she was turned, her legs were straightened, and her feet pressed snugly against the blocks, to keep them at right angles. Her fists were so tight that she was cutting the palms of her hands with her fingernails. Large wads of gauze bandage were tied into her hands to keep the fingers semiextended.

She moved frequently, primarily from involuntary muscle contractions but partly from what I believed to be deliberate voluntary actions. It was impossible to keep anything in position for any appreciable length of time. It added to her routine care; hand pads had to be repositioned, legs straightened, feet braced. Those tendons could not be permitted to shrink.

Dr. Holtzman, director of the rehabilitation department, was called to evaluate her. I did not see him at that time and learned only later that he had grave misgivings about her ability to recover. He agreed, however, to let a physical therapist try to work with her.

Raleigh Johnston was to treat her twice a day. I liked her from the first moment I met her. She was a lovely young girl with the face and patience of a small blond angel. Her eyes radiated confidence; her voice sparked enthusiasm.

She manipulated each joint, from toes to neck, keeping a full range of motion. She was trying to prevent Ginny's limbs from tightening so badly that she would never be able to straighten them again. She taught me how to do the exercises and it finally gave me something that would have a positive effect on Gin's recovery— something *I* could do.

Each time I visited I would go through the whole routine. Her joints were so tight that I was afraid of dislocating something. Frequently, I'd try my own arm to see if a shoulder really could move that far, before I'd try to force Ginny's.

After two days it became apparent that the exercises could not prevent distortion of her arms and legs. Two orthopedic men, Drs. Linwood and Kozinn, came to examine her. I was not there at the time, so they left the message with the nurses. On the following day, they would apply four lightweight casts to keep her wrists and ankles in the correct position.

Next morning I came to visit, forgetting that Dr. Linwood would have worked on her. I came into her room full of my "new day" optimism. One look at her and I felt that someone had plunged a knife into my heart. For me, this was the most difficult day. Maybe it was because I had forgotten that it was to happen and had not steeled myself to face it. It seemed so pathetic, I found myself biting my lip to keep from crying.

She was so frail, so completely helpless. She could hardly move her arms or legs. How awful that such torturous monstrosities were necessary. The longer I looked at them, the huger they grew. I couldn't even talk to her, because I knew my voice would crack, and I would start to cry. I could not let her know that my confidence had a breaking point. I just stood by her bed and held her hand. My heart was crying, "Ginny, Ginny, won't it ever get any easier for you?"

Finally I lifted one leg. The cast was cold and hard. Maybe, medically, they were considered "lightweight," but they seemed such a burden for those thin little legs. How would she ever be able to move her limbs dragging all that bulk?

Without warning, a very close friend, a Capuchin Brother, walked into her room. He had come to visit Ginny, but I think God sent him to give me back my courage.

He saw the casts and remarked that no one had told him she had broken her arms or legs. I explained the reason for the casts, their therapeutic value, the fact that casts applied now would enable her to walk later. Explaining it to him, I convinced myself.

That brief moment of doubt and despair made me realize how fortunate I had been that God had given me the faith to face everything else. Faith must be an outright gift from God. If it were humanly possible to summon it within ourselves, I should have been able to grasp it that morning. But, I could not. Had it been out of reach for a moment, just to intensify my total dependence on Him?

I had been trying to learn all the doctors' names, and what each one was doing for her. The nurses knew of my efforts and would alert me as one approached the room. For all their tutoring, I would still get them confused, calling one doctor by another's name—but they seemed to understand.

When Dr. Metcalf said that all the work would be covered by specialists, I had no comprehension of how many he was talking about.

It was a vast crew. There were three pediatricians, four neurosurgeons, one chest specialist, one pediatric surgeon, two orthopedic doctors, two urologists and the anesthesiologist who still checked on her. Counting Dr. Metcalf, a total of fifteen doctors were actually working on her. The doctor who had been at the scene of the accident stopped in whenever he was on the floor. The house pediatrician frequently visited her. Often, there were doctors whose identification I never learned who I imagine were "just checking."

When the bandage was originally put on, Ginny's head was swollen. As the swelling started to go down, the bandage slipped closer to her eyes. It soon looked like a little face, dwarfed by an oversized white football helmet.

Dan and I came in one evening and the change in her appearance was startling. The bandage had been removed. The nurses had replaced it with a white cotton knit cap that made her look like a pixie.

They asked if we wanted to see her head. You don't . . . and you do. The cap was removed and I was amazed how smooth her head looked. She now had a little fuzz regrown. All the scars were in back of the hairline and would eventually be covered. The skin was still black, blue and yellow from the bruising. But, all in all, it was far better than I expected.

Sometime afterward, I noticed the scalp pulsating and got up the courage to run my hand over her head. Her little skull felt like broken rocks. The pulsating was over the holes that were left where all the broken chips of bone had been cleared away. Dr. Burstein assured me that it was perfectly safe, that there would be no need to put a plate over it.

I was relieved that she might not have to endure anything more, but it seemed so fragile and tender.

I don't know exactly when we started to get other people to believe that she was understanding. It was easier to convince the nurses than the doctors that we were getting positive responses. There were times when a definite understanding lighted that one eye. So many times, she would move a leg or an arm when asked. Finally one of the doctors agreed with us and ordered a television brought into her room. He felt she was hearing. There should be something for her to hear. The nurses asked for a list of her favorite TV shows and taped it to the set insuring its being kept on the proper channel.

Although she was improving in so many ways, still there was no sound. Nothing. Not a sigh or a whimper. The "speech center" was in the area of the severest injury to her brain, but I still kept telling myself that it just needed a little more healing.

After all the noise of eight children, it was incredible that I would stand by her bed and pray that she would cry. But, that I did. I prayed for a word, a noise, a grunt—any sound—any hope that there was some voice left.

From all the grimaces she would make, keeping the range of motion in her joints must have been very painful. The most painful was obviously when Raleigh would stretch her "hamstrings." She would straighten Ginny's knee and rest her foot on her own shoulder, then lift till the leg was at right angles with her body. Then one glorious day Raleigh forced the leg and Ginny let out a painful little wail! Every nurse on the floor was in the room in seconds. Ginny cried again—and we all cried together. Tears of joy are sweet, unashamed!

I kept wondering how we would know when she was completely out of the coma. I had reasoned that as long as she was still in it, we could attribute inabilities to her being semiconscious, and had more progress to anticipate as part of regaining consciousness. If she were medically out of the coma, then this helpless little being was all that was left.

Expecting the doctors or nurses to commit themselves as to her level of consciousness, I repeatedly asked, "How do you know when she is fully out of the coma?" Invariably, they replied, "You'll know before we do. You know her better than any of us. You'll recognize the signs of consciousness. You'll know."

I had always thought a person came out of a coma dramatically, with the doctor triumphantly striding out of the room announcing, "The crisis is over!"

This obviously was not going to happen. I had seen signs of understanding. Were these the signs they meant? Was she really conscious and were all these weaknesses a result of the injury? I wanted them to tell me, "She is still unconscious, so her greatest progress is yet to come." But, no one would give any pronouncement—one way or the other.

Finally, Dr. Rosenzweig, one of the pediatricians, explained that it was a "wavelike" pattern of healing. There was a little more consciousness and a slipping back. There was another improvement and another plateau. There were times when she was "conscious," others when she was completely out. So, whether or not she was out of the coma depended on the moment of the day. As far as knowing when she would be fully conscious, all of the time, there was no way of knowing. It could be days, or months, depending mostly on the length of the plateaus . . . and they were unpredictable.

Since it was somewhat up to me to make the decision, I leaned heavily on her still being in the coma. I was sure that she was going to recover, and one day she would "wake up."

But for all my confidence, we really knew so little. We could see the healing of Ginny's bruises and scrapes, but we didn't know what was going on inside her head.

Dan mentioned this to Dr. Rosenzweig, and once more, he took medical information and translated it into a layman's terms.

"You can see how the bruises around her eyes are healing. The change has been slow, but apparent. That same healing is taking place in her brain. It has been severely bruised, but it is slowly healing, just as the external bruises are. If you watch the recovery in these bruises which you can see, you have a pretty good idea of the amount of healing that has taken place inside."

His explanation gave us another cause to believe there would be more improvements. Her eyes were still badly bruised; her brain must be also. There would be more healing in that little head; greater recovery was still to come.

After three weeks, Jeanne was well enough to go home. She still wanted to see Ginny and thought that as long as she was out of traction, she might be allowed to visit. There was no way of explaining that you really did not "visit" with Ginny. To another child, particularly one so involved, Ginny's appearance and treatment could be so frightening that it might leave Jeanne terribly upset. Her mother, the nurses and I all agreed it was better she did not see Ginny.

Just before Jeanne left, a friend visited her and brought a doll for each little girl in the room. In all the excitement, one little girl went home without hers. It was returned to Jeanne. Instead of being delighted to have "twin dolls," she asked the nurse to please give it to Ginny.

Jeanne's friend was teasing with her, "If you could have anything in the world right now, if I could give you anything at all, what would you really want?"

"I'd like Ginny to get all better."

And so she left for home, saddened because she could not see her little friend.

❉❉❉

CHAPTER 6

ONE AFTERNOON, GINNY WAS "RESTING" MORE THAN USUAL. I WAS SIT-
ting by her bed, deep in thought. As I am prone to do when completely absorbed in a problem, I was frowning, staring into space.
Diane Paquet, one of the nurses, observed it, came into the room,
made some superfluous checks on the equipment, then sat down to
talk.

Though she had not yet started on a family of her own, she had
a motherly manner, a mixture of love, humor and plain common
sense, which she lavished on Gin. She felt that at the moment, however, I needed more care than Ginny. She understood how exceed-
ingly difficult it was, how empty the words "just wait and see." She
counseled, "Try to be patient. I know it's hard, waiting without
knowing what to expect. Just because the doctors must be so pes-
simistic, you can't give up. Ginny needs you to keep believing in
her."

It was good that she had not come on a day I was feeling depressed. She was so sincere that I'm afraid on a day of lesser faith
I would have gone to pieces. At that particular time, I was just exhausted and mulling it all over in my mind. It was good to talk with
her, and it was quite apparent that she had become deeply attached
to Ginny. In trying to encourage me, she was bolstering her own
confidence.

We were beginning to have cause for confidence. Things were
now stabilizing to a point that Ginny's vital signs were checked
only on the hour! It was interesting that things were evaluated in
light of the incidents surrounding them. If the injury had been

slight, and vital signs were checked hourly, I would have been alarmed by the necessity for such intense care. Under these circumstances, the same fact was encouraging rather than disturbing.

It was now about three and a half weeks that Ginny's temperature was kept low by the "ice blanket." The cotton blanket that covered the plastic was constantly getting soaked with condensation. She was "turned" every hour. Each time the nurses would have to change the entire bed. They just would not let her lie on a damp blanket. They felt it necessary to protect her skin, and "it's bad enough that she's 'freezing,' she doesn't have to be wet besides." It took time to change all that linen, but it was always done cheerfully and lovingly. No effort was too much if it made her more comfortable.

The nurses used to joke about the reason for the "ice blanket" treatment. They said it must be so miserable sleeping on that cold, clammy surface that a patient would get up and walk just to get away from it. Their teasing was confirmed by a friend of mine who had a brain tumor removed. After surgery, she, too, was treated with an "ice blanket." She said it was horrible. "I was never so cold in my life. I'm sure they make you lie on that thing just so your head feels good by comparison."

Most of the nurses were young, but there was one exception, a grandmotherly woman who was considerably older. Ginny became her special love. She mentioned her concern that she was becoming too attached to Ginny, but, hard as she would try, she couldn't help it.

One day, as she was caring for Gin, we started to talk. She didn't seem to have her usual high spirits. I wondered what was troubling her. It seemed that for some reason she was losing confidence in herself and I couldn't understand why. She was so capable, and had a tenderness and understanding enriched by experience.

Not having any children of their own, she and her husband evidently had been exceptionally close and dependent on each other. He had died a few years before, and at times it seemed that life had no purpose without him.

I asked her if possibly she was placed here to help save Ginny's life? The attachment grew deeper—and for the whole time Ginny was in the hospital, she walked a little straighter, with a little more bounce in her step.

The most important thing is life is simply to be needed!

The blow to Ginny's head was so severe that it had completely upset her body's temperature-control system. The machine had to be adjusted frequently because her temperature would rise and fall unpredictably. It took twenty-five days for her temperature to stabilize.

One morning when I came in, her room was strangely quiet. The hum of the "refrigerator" was missing! I took her hand and it was warm! For the first time in almost a month, she felt alive!

The first stretch was short. Her temperature started to climb. She had to be cooled down again. Each time, they were able to leave it off a little longer. Each day was a little better.

After several days, one of the nurses who had worked so intensely with Ginny, came down the hall to meet me, bubbling over with excitement. "Guess what! She's been off it for almost six hours!"

As we walked down the corridor, she told me she had a little sister about the same age as Ginny. She had been telling her family about Gin and the little girl promised when she made her First Communion on the following Saturday, she would offer it just for Ginny!

By Saturday, Ginny was off the "ice blanket" completely!

More equipment was moved out! The nicest thing about this progress was that, for the first time in a full month, she could wear pajamas! Just the warmth of a cotton shirt had been too much for her body to control. Now, she was dressed and the screen was removed from her door!

As Ginny gained consciousness, it was decided that the time had come for her to relearn to eat. The excitement and preparations were comparable to those of a great banquet. Her head tended to roll to one side; her neck did not have the strength or control to hold it straight. It would have been more difficult for her to swallow that way, so her head was propped with a little folded pillow. The bed was rolled up till she was half-sitting. Her napkin was a clean diaper, tucked all around her shoulders. No one mentioned it, but it seemed expected that she would vomit and they were trying to be ready for it.

Her "meal" arrived—a Dixie cup of vanilla ice cream. The nurse took just a drop on the end of the spoon and placed it on her tongue. She swallowed! Another bit—another success. Little by little, she ate what amounted to almost a teaspoonful of ice cream. She was watched carefully. There was a risk that it would be forced out through the tracheotomy. That stayed clear and the ice cream stayed down!

I was overjoyed! On the way out of the hospital, I saw a nurse I knew who worked in the operating room. I had to stop her and tell the wonderful news. She already knew. In fact, she said the whole hospital knew five minutes after Ginny had eaten. She had become the pet and special hope of everyone who worked there. From maintenance men to doctors there was a bond of concern for "that little girl who was hurt so badly." They all checked on her progress and each gain gave them added hope and enthusiasm.

Whenever I returned home, I was always greeted by the other children with, "What did Ginny do today?"

They must have known by the bounce in my step and the look on my face that it had been good. I told them, "Ginny ate ice cream."

Bernadette, getting just as skeptical as the doctors, questioned, "Did she eat it with her mouth, or did they melt it and put it in her 'tube'?"

Thanksgiving was going to be difficult for my brother Joe and his children without Nancy, and for us without Ginny. My mother and father thought it best if we all came and had dinner with them. The complete confusion of mixing two large families together made it difficult to check on who was there—and who wasn't.

Afterward, Mom and Dad kept all fourteen children and Joe came with us to visit Ginny. It was the first time he had seen her, but he had been told of her progress. He explained how her improvements were similar, but the reverse of what he had watched with Nancy—she slipping toward death—and Ginny climbing away from it.

Throughout the whole time, I leaned heavily on Joe's example. Through Nancy's sickness and death, he had such patience; always seemed so full of hope and good spirits. I felt that if Joe had such faith and self-control when he had less hope every day, I had no right to complain or despair when I had reason for more hope each day!

Just after Thanksgiving, about six weeks after the accident, I was rubbing lotion on Ginny to keep her skin from breaking down and noticed a small pimple on the back of her leg. I had never seen a bedsore—and now was afraid to ask.

One of my sisters-in-law had made a date with me to have lunch, then visit Ginny. I was late in meeting her train, so I left the hospital without having a chance to mention the sore to one of the nurses.

After the strenuous time we had had, it was delightful to relax over a luncheon. I completely forgot about that one little pimple.

When we arrived back at Ginny's room, the door was closed. The head nurse called me aside. (How frightening the closed room and her gravity as she separated me from the other visitors.) With a controlled calmness, she began, "Mrs. Carson, I must tell you something. I'm very sorry . . . Ginny has the chicken pox."

I had been terrified that she had had a relapse—or worse. Now, I was so relieved it was a strain to keep from laughing out loud. The sudden release made me giddy.

Only three months before, one of the nurses in the maternity ward was explaining to me that when you have a sick child, you do not have to spread it around the whole family. You simply isolate the child—keep dishes, clothing, bedding, etc. all separate, and you have just one sick child. I listened politely to her instruction, and wondered how the system would work when she married and had a houseful of her own children.

Evidently it was a theory that worked in textbooks, but not in practice. In spite of hospital precautions, one little patient, who was innocently carrying it, spread chicken pox all over the pediatrics ward before anyone even knew she had it. It even spread to patients in isolation, where dishes, clothing, bedding, etc., had all been kept separate. Dr. Ronis told me a story of chicken pox spreading through four floors of a hospital, up the heating ducts!

And, if there can be a bright side to chicken pox, Ginny was quite unconscious and consequently not as itchy as she would have been normally. I mentioned this to Dr. Gelfand and he said, "Better that her brain was healed—and she could scratch!"

We went in to see her, after scrubbing and donning sterile gowns. She was in strict isolation. There were only a few spots. I hoped it would be a light case. But, the next day there were more —then more—till there wasn't an unblemished area two inches square. I counted thirty-seven pox on one finger, and half the finger was covered by the cast!

It also gave me a little insight into the intensity with which specialists work. Each has his own "field" and lets the others work on their area. One of the neurosurgeons came in, examined her head (which had not yet broken out with the pox) and asked why she had been isolated. He never noticed that the rest of her body was covered with the pox.

It was probably a record duration for chicken pox. Many of the sores were so deep that they filled with blood. After covering the rest of her body, they spread all over her head and face, into her hair and eyebrows, inside her ears—and something of a last straw, they even developed on her eyelids!

During this whole period, there was only one evening when she seemed restless from the itching, and was given a sedative. Otherwise, because she was only semiconscious, the pox did not seem to bother her as much as they did anyone observing her. Sores eventually started to scab, making her appearance even worse. Once they were fully scabbed, however, it was no longer contagious and the isolation was discontinued.

The chicken pox did accomplish something. There was some concern, mostly on my part, as to the condition of the sores that were covered by the casts. I reasoned that if the exposed sores were so deep, the incubated ones must be monstrous.

It was agreed to remove the casts to give the pox underneath a chance to heal. I still disliked those casts, even though I kept reminding myself they were for an ultimate good. I was happy to see Dr. Kozinn arrive with his little electric saw. Ginny was confused by the noise and by my covering her face with a diaper to keep the dust out of her eyes. In a few minutes it was over. Her legs were spindly and festered, but the sores were not quite as bad as I had anticipated. She seemed relieved with the freedom—although it was only intermittent.

The casts were bivalved—carefully cut down both sides making two shells, like an oyster's. They could then be taken off for part of the day, particularly for therapy, and replaced for the remainder of the time by tightly wrapping the two sections with bandage. This gave her ankles the support they still needed, but allowed more freedom to exercise.

Raleigh had been doing "range-of-motion" exercises with Ginny eleven times a week. Now, she came into her room and announced brightly, "Let's try to sit her up today." I was somewhat astonished, but it seemed like great progress and I was willing to help any way that I could.

We lifted those little legs over the side of the bed and slowly righted her to a sitting postion. I thought she was going to pass out. There was absolutely no balance. She turned white and started to cry. She was up for only a fraction of a second, but it was a tremendous stride.

Each session, from then on, we'd keep her up just a little longer; each time it would get easier. There still was no balance, but it seemed to get less and less painful for her.

All through those weeks, how thoughtful the nurses were. One day Diane asked, "How would you like to hold her?"

At first I could not comprehend all that she was implying. When I finally understood, I couldn't believe it.

We borrowed a chair, with arms, from the solarium. Extra pillows were brought from the linen closet. Her catheter was attached to a leg bag. Diane got me thoroughly braced and comfortable in the chair, then lifted Ginny, so gently, out of bed and put her in my arms. There are no words to describe how wonderful it was! As soon as we were both perfectly safe, she left us. I sang to Gin for a while, then she relaxed, completely content, and went to sleep. It was the sweetest time in many, many weeks.

I don't know how much good it did Ginny, but it did wonders for me!

There is something soothing about a mother being able to hold a hurt child in her arms. It seems to form a shield from any further harm and remove some of the sting from all the past hurt. Without words, it seems to say—and be understood and believed—"Everything is going to be all right."

✳ ✳ ✳

CHAPTER 7

THE SWELLING IN GINNY'S LEFT EYE WAS SUBSIDING. THE COLORATION had varied from black to purple to green to yellow, and now she looked like a child who had discovered and experimented with eye shadow. The eye now looked more "painted" than injured. Then it finally started to open. It was again obvious that it was injured. She was unable to fuse the vision of both eyes. The muscles just could not control the movements of the left eye. It would move around searchingly—apparently unable to see. Soon she learned to use only the right eye, and could focus and see with that one alone. It relieved the confusion she seemed to have in trying to use both eyes together.

The left eye had been injured so seriously, that previously I had wondered if she still had that eye. Now I was relieved to know the eye was there, but her difficulty in using it made me wonder about its ability to function. Again, I tried to convince myself that it just needed a little more time to heal.

Soon I realized that occasionally she was able to isolate the use of the left eye, just as she had been doing with the right eye. She could not look at something with both eyes, but was able to use each independently. There had to be vision in the left eye! Now it was just a case of her relearning to use them together. After some of the other things she had accomplished, that seemed quite simple and minor, and I felt confident that her vision soon would be restored. Ignorance was bliss.

Little by little, that first bit of ice cream was increased, till she was able to eat a whole Dixie cup at a time. Next she was started on cereal and baby food. There were three "meals" a day, and be-tween-meal "snacks" to supplement the instant breakfast that was still poured into the gastrostomy. It took a long time to feed her, since she could take only a tiny bit at a time. It meant a nurse could be tied up for almost an hour, feeding her. I tried to get there in time for lunch to relieve them. Besides, I enjoyed doing it. It was a delight to see her eat. She loved music, and I'd often sing to her when I fed her. It was a pleasant time for both of us.

Drinking was a little more difficult. Just as a baby has difficulty keeping liquids in its mouth, and swallowing them before they run out, she had trouble relearning the oral movements necessary to get the milk down her throat rather than down her chin. There was no way we could explain how to swallow, so we just kept working at it, sip by sip, one-half ounce at a time, using a little medicine cup the size of a shot glass. She liked to eat and worked diligently at mastering the art.

Before long, Ginny was eating quite a full, well-balanced meal of baby meat, vegetable and mashed potatoes. If the kitchen had forgotten the condiments, thinking the tray was for a baby, the nurses always made sure she had butter, pepper and salt, com-menting, "As long as she can eat, it at least should taste good."

One evening when we visited, Dan said to her, "Mommy said you ate such a good lunch today. Do you remember how you used to show me how much you had eaten?"

She opened her mouth wide so he could "see"!

She had to be remembering! If Dan had asked her to open her mouth, it could have been a direct response to a command. But, he had carefully phrased the question so that her response could leave no doubt that she had memory going back prior to the accident.

"Dear God, thank you again."

Her intake was recorded down to the last half ounce, and ac-curate records were kept on her weight gain. (The nurses threat-ened to keep weight records on me as well. I had lost twenty pounds in the last two months and they seemed just as concerned about my loss as hers.) She started to regain the weight. As the oral intake was increased, the liquid through the gastrostomy was decreased.

Finally she could take enough by mouth so that the tube could be removed from her stomach.

At the time he had originally done the operation, Dr. Noto explained how it was all put in—an incision in both the abdominal wall and the stomach, the suturing of the stomach to the abdominal wall to keep it open and the insertion of the tube.

It may have been simple for him, but it sounded very complicated to me and I expected another operation, the whole procedure in reverse, to remove the tube.

One day I arrived just as he was leaving her room. He had taken it out right there and simply put a light bandage over it.

I was amazed and asked how all that could be done so readily; would it heal that easily?

He smiled and said simply, "God is good!"

Even though the nurses assured me it was possible to speak with a tracheotomy, I was trying to convince myself that the metal tube in her throat was obstructing her speech. I had been hoping and praying fervently that when the tube was finally removed it would release her voice.

One evening while we were alone with Ginny, Dan and I experimented by covering the opening in her throat. It didn't have any effect on Gin's inability to speak but we did make a discovery. She could breathe through her mouth without any difficulty!

We told the nurses and they repeated the experiment. They agreed she seemed to have no difficulty breathing normally, so they relayed this information to the doctors and the decision was made to remove the tracheotomy.

I was visiting with her when Dr. Gelfand arrived to do the job. In good humor he quipped, "Nurse, just bring that book in here and keep it open to the right page, so I know what I'm doing."

I had no idea how I would react, so even though he did not ask me to, I decided it was better that I go for a walk in the hall.

In a few minutes he was finished and chided me, "If I had known it was going to be frightening, I would have left with you." It is good for the soul to be able to laugh when the heart wants to cry.

I went back to her room, praying almost as desperately as that first day, "Dear God, please. . . ."

I took her hand, "Hi, Ginny." My heart was aching to hear, "Hi, Mommy" . . . but there was no sound.

The only real change was that the metal plate on her throat was replaced by a small white bandage. I noticed another difference, however, for which I could get no support. While the tracheotomy was in, she always held her head to one side. As part of the range-of-motion exercises, her head was rotated to keep the neck muscles free. Whenever it was done, she grimaced. I felt that the tube in her throat must have irritated her every time they moved her head. Now that the tube was gone, she no longer made the faces, and started moving her head on her own. This, however, was another thing that fell into the category of "it might be—but it could just be coincidence."

Finally the catheter was removed. Now, almost two months after the accident, Ginny was functioning entirely on her own again!

* * *

CHAPTER 8

WE REARRANGED HER ROOM FOR TWO REASONS. FIRST, IT WAS FELT that since all the action in the room was on her right side, that might have been the reason she always held her head to the right. By putting her bed against the other wall, it encouraged her to turn her head. The tracheotomy was removed just after the turning of the bed, so no one ever decided if it was the removal of the tube, the moving of the center of interest or the increased facility of the neck muscles that caused her to turn her head.

The second reason was simply to please her. At home, Ginny liked nothing better than rearranging her room. But here in the hospital, with only a bed, a table, a chair and a TV in a small room, there were few alternate arrangements. We tried several new ways —aiming at the ultimate in efficiency for the nurses, and comfort and view for her.

Just before Christmas, I was holding her when Dan stopped on his way home from work. He observed that it would be easier for her to see the TV if it was moved, and started pushing it to a new location. Just as I was cautioning him to be careful of the toys on top, her doll toppled to the floor . . . and Ginny chuckled!

"Dan, she laughed!" The tears filled my eyes.

He was more cautious than I, and warned me that we could be mistaken; maybe she had just coughed and I thought she had laughed. I was so positive that by the time we were home, I convinced him to such a degree that it warranted a whole round of phone calls to let everyone know the wonderful progress.

The following day, Diane was with us in the room. Dan was explaining the incident to her. She could be quite a clown and put on a "one-man show" for Ginny.

Ginny definitely laughed!

Diane interrupted her act—turned to me and said, "Merry Christmas, mother!"

I couldn't thank her, or return the good wishes. My throat was choked and the tears were streaming down my face.

Now that Ginny was no longer "contagious" from chicken pox, Raleigh suggested that we start taking her down to the therapy department for her daily sessions. There were several objectives. First, the varied equipment available downstairs would afford an increased program of therapy. Secondly, the change of scene would be good for her increasing awareness.

It was quite a routine to take her. Getting her into a bathrobe and onto a stretcher was the beginning. On the preliminary excursions a nurse accompanied me, but after a few trips they trusted me to take her on my own. I never did learn how to manipulate a stretcher through swinging doors, gracefully, but as long as her hands were tucked safely inside, I could do little more damage than chipping some paint.

The whole activity of the trip, twice a day, was good for her. It broke up the day, previously spent entirely in one room.

At the therapy department, they were able to use the "mats"— low, padded bedlike frames, six feet square. Now there was room to begin teaching her to roll over. Rolling over was something every other child in the family had simply done as an infant. I never realized just how complicated it was to explain, nor how much training it took to "teach" a helpless child the whole process.

Raleigh's patience and encouragement were boundless! And they needed to be. I had no idea that each physical accomplishment was going to take months of hard work.

With Christmas approaching, in their spare time, and frequently on their own time after hours, the nurses started decorating the whole ward. They offered to do Ginny's room, but thought it might mean more to her if we brought decorations from home which she might recognize.

Years before, I had made a detailed cutout of the Nativity that we used on the front door. It had become a "family tradition" on December 8, the Feast of the Immaculate Conception, that the picture was brought from the attic, carefully unwrapped and hung on the door.

The children all agreed, if there was a chance Ginny would recognize anything, that would be the best choice. They decided Ginny should have it for that Christmas. Whether or not she was aware or saw well enough to recognize it, we didn't know.

One of the nurses brought a tiny artificial tree, set it up on her bedside table and decorated it just for her.

The solarium, which in the children's ward is known as the "porch" was the general play area for all the ambulatory patients. The nurses got a big tree, and did a fine job trimming it. A life-sized, red velvet Santa was brought out of storage. He came down the hall, prone, on the shoulders of two maintenance men. The first glimpse was a little unnerving. They could have at least put him on a stretcher.

The porch was so festive that one of the evening nurses felt it was not fair that Ginny could not see it. It was generally crowded with parents and patients during visiting hours. The nurse asked us to wait one evening, until the other visitors had left, and she had most of the children settled for the night.

She came back to Ginny's room, pulling a stretcher. Dan lifted Gin onto it, and we all went out to see the big tree and the Santa. While we were talking to Ginny, the nurse disappeared down the hall. She came back with a tray of ice cream and soda so Ginny would have a "Christmas party."

So many times the nurses took extra time and trouble to do "special" things for her. None of them were necessary for her physical care . . . but they were vitally important for her spirits. She would not be going home in a few days, as most of the patients were; they would do all they could to make her prolonged stay as pleasant and "special" as they possibly could. They never neglected their other patients, but used free moments—and sometimes I'm sure those "moments" were the time they would have had for a cup of coffee. But they all loved her and took it upon themselves as a special assignment to do everything possible to "make Ginny well."

The hospital regulations specified that no child under sixteen was allowed to visit. None of our other children were old enough, so for two months they had only our reports of Ginny's progress.

Christmas was going to be empty without her. I kept trying to conceive an idea that would allow some of them to visit. One day I cornered Dr. Rosenzweig and put it to him. "Would it be possible to bring some of the older children to visit Ginny, Christmas afternoon? The ward will be empty; any child that possibly can, will have been sent home. There would be little risk of contagion—either way."

He was sober. "Those rules are made for good reasons. I don't think it would be at all advisable to take the risk. No, I'm sorry, but I just could not give you permission to bring them in here."

My heart sank. It had seemed a possibility of partially bringing the family together for Christmas. Now the chance was shattered.

He sensed my disappointment—and brightened. "But, you know, she is allowed out of her room. I'll arrange for you to use the assembly room, downstairs, and give permission for Ginny to go down that afternoon. Then you will be able to bring as many of the children as you want. There are no age restrictions down there."

My spirits flew from the depths to the heights. That Christmas was the merriest, most blessed and meaningful, we had ever known!

Dan's mother and brother started the day with us. We all went to Mass together—even Roberta, who normally spent Mass time asleep in her crib. The other children were in a turmoil about whether she would be a good girl. "What are you going to do if she cries?" To satisfy them, I had a warmed bottle tucked in my pocketbook. She behaved better than some of the ones that were fidgeting, to see if she was being good.

More than ever, I was concerned about Ginny's speech. When it did not return with the removal of the tracheotomy, I still clung to the hope that it could come back spontaneously. I reasoned that if something tremendous triggered it, she could just start to talk.

I prayed desperately all through Mass. "Dear God, please . . will you do it?" Certainly the first visit of all those children would be the biggest "excitement" she would experience. Maybe . . .

Then all my hopes swung away. Were we making a terrible mistake taking the children to see her? Would she even know them? Would the confusion be too much for her—and possibly cause a setback? How would it affect the other children? Had we over-played her little improvements? Would they be shocked by her appearance or dismayed by her helplessness?

The pendulum swung back again. Maybe it would be rough on all of us, but if it could release her speech, the final result would be worth it. It was obvious to me that her mind was bursting with things she wanted to tell us—questions she wanted to ask—and they were all locked inside.

"Dear God, you've done so much for her already. You can do it. Please, oh please, let her talk again."

We arrived at the assembly room, filled with a mixture of ex-citement and apprehension—the excitement mostly from the younger ones, the apprehension from the older children.

Dan and Mom got the children settled. For some of them, it was the first time they had been inside a hospital, and they were some-what awe-struck.

I went upstairs to get Ginny. We had gotten candy-striped paja-mas that had a matching granny cap, to cover the little fuzz and long scars on her head. She was ready to go. I had no idea how much she understood of all I had been telling her about visiting the other children. I started to take her down alone, but two of the nurses who could be spared from the ward insisted on going with me. Were they hoping for the same miracle—or was it just that they wanted to see the rest of the family?

My anxiety made the trip seem long. As we neared the room, I could hear the children talking in hushed voices. It would be the first time they had seen their little sister in two long full months.

They all started to talk at once. "Hi, Ginny." "Ginny, how are you?" "Remember us?" "Are you getting all better?" "Can you come home soon?"

They were all talking . . . but she was silent. I had asked for too big a miracle.

But the visit went well. She smiled and laughed. She remembered them and was obviously delighted to see them. The children did beautifully. They joked and played with her, then exhibited a ma-turity I hadn't expected. They were filled with other questions that, somehow, they knew were better saved for the trip home. "Why does she look different?" "Why can't she—?" "Will she ever—?"

Dan took pictures, and there was a competition as to who would be closest to her. The expressions on their faces were unforgettable —the love, compassion and tenderness they radiated!

We laid Roberta in the stretcher with Ginny's arm around her— the children all gathered around—and my heart was bursting. Was there ever more peace on earth or good will between brothers and sisters?

We came home for dinner. Because of the strain the last two months had been for the children, everyone lavished gifts on them. Our living room looked like an explosion in a toy factory.

That evening, when Dan and I went to visit Ginny, we took some of the turkey dinner we had at home. After much mashing and cutting, I got it fine enough so that Ginny could eat it. Not only had the children visited with her, but she shared dinner with us.

It had been the happiest day in a long time.

* * *

CHAPTER 9

After Christmas, Ginny started one of those plateaus that the doctors had warned me about. She had had some earlier, but they lasted only a day or two. This one seemed to go on and on. When anyone wanted to know how she was coming along, it was difficult to find progress to claim. I'd keep looking for little signs of improvement, wondering if this was to be the last plateau. It had been so many weeks, without any concrete hope. Was this the end of the road? Her condition was far from promising, but something kept me from giving up.

Sometimes people questioned why we kept driving ourselves that hard to spend every available minute with her. There were many days when I was exhausted; days when the housework was piled so high that it was impossible to see any way of ever catching up. Yet, I could not stay home. Each time she had progressed, each stride . . . the first cry . . . the first laugh . . . had always come when we were with her.

Many days during that long plateau, it seemed I had accomplished nothing tangible for my efforts, but hope kept urging me to try again the next day. My visits with Ginny were possible only because so many gave their time.

Alice had taken on the responsibility of being my "social secretary." Right after the accident, she had called many of the women in the neighborhood and arranged a schedule. Each one offered to take care of the rest of my family one day a week so that I was free to spend midmorning to midafternoon with Ginny. Each evening, my father would care for the children to let Dan and me go together.

The hours these friends spent taking care of the children were uncountable. Not one ever complained—not one ever made me feel that I was imposing upon them. In their own way, they were "helping Ginny get better."

Most of the baby sitters kept the children at their own homes. There was, however, one exception—Mrs. Clancy. Her own children were all grown, and it was easier for her to come to us. Her jovial manner and appearance tempted the children to nickname her "Mrs. Santa Claus." Though that name was accurate, we decided "Auntie Clancy" was more appropriate.

My kitchen and living room seemed to present a challenge to her. My normal morning chores usually lasted till about ten in the evening . . . on the better days. As hard as I would try to get the wash done, the kitchen cleaned up and the living room tidy, I never made it. It never seemed to faze her a bit. When I came home from the hospital, the mountains of "important papers" that accumulated from school had disappeared, the disorder was gone. (I still don't know what she did with it. Nothing was ever missing— but it wasn't there.) The table was always set for dinner. Supper was often cooked; she'd have made a cake or left dessert chilling in the refrigerator. She could make any meal look like an artistic creation.

Mrs. Clancy did one special favor for me. The day before the accident, Ginny had picked a bouquet of flowers in the garden and arranged them in a little vase in the center of the kitchen table. The flowers died. In those first fearsome days, I could not throw out those dead flowers. In tidying up, Mrs. Clancy had not recognized their significance and thought I just hadn't gotten around to discarding them. She replaced them with fresh ones. It sounds ridiculously philosophical over a little bunch of flowers, but it seemed to remove the fear of death and replace it with more hope for new life.

Often, friends would stop in while I was at the hospital. I'd come home to a pan of lasagna, meat loaf, soup, spaghetti sauce, anything that could be cooked and moved readily. The food would be left—often with a little note—"Thought you might not feel like cooking tonight."

Alice was wonderful beyond description. When it was her day, she would not wait for me to bring the children to her. I'd come downstairs, after having changed the baby, to find Alice finishing the breakfast dishes. She would have a bottle warmed and say, "You start the wash; I'll feed the baby. She eats better for me than she does for you, anyway." As much as she disliked my system for making formula, she learned how and would have it started. She knew better how to run my kitchen than I did.

I had grown so close to Alice, and she was so perceptive, that she seemed to understand me completely. She knew my highs and my lows, my hopes and my fears. She knew when it was good to talk—and when it was better to keep silent. Having Alice for a friend was one of the greatest good fortunes of my life.

Her influence spread. Not only did I have "baby sitters," but whenever I needed a ride, she knew who had a car available. My ironing was picked up and delivered, shopping done and errands run. The help even reached my pile of mending. One neighbor delivered a box of cookies and mentioned, "I just finished lengthening dresses for my granddaughters. You must have some that need to be done," and went home to alter hems that I just could never seem to get done.

The only one who ever "gave up" on helping was one neighbor who started folding my basket of socks. Because of school uniforms, all the children wore navy blue socks. After lining up twenty socks and not finding a pair, she was getting discouraged. I asked her what she'd do if she did find a pair? Ten of the feet were all the same size. How would she know whose it was? She decided it would be better if I folded the socks. She'd wash the dishes.

All of their kindness I'm sure God counted as special prayers for Ginny's recovery.

Many friends and relatives had Masses offered, but one of the most touching incidents occurred when one of the secretaries at the hospital stopped me one day. She seemed a little uneasy, as if she did not know quite where to begin. "I know that you are Catholic, and I hope you won't mind, but I told the Rabbi about Ginny. Prayers for her recovery were asked at our synagogue. Rather than have a Mass said, this seemed better to me, because this is what I believe myself."

I was touched. What could help the cause of ecumenism more

than all faiths praying for the same little girl? We agreed that it was simply different roads to the same God.

Ginny's room might have properly been called the "intensive care unit" of pediatrics. But the nurses, I learned one day, referred to it by a different name. They called it their "Miracle Room."

When I brought Ginny back from therapy one day, Diane announced that we'd have to start packing. Ginny was being moved to the large room across the hall! I probably should have had more concern for the new patient coming in, but I was too wrapped up in my own happiness. For the first time in two and a half months, Ginny was not the sickest child in the ward!

The little boy who took her room had to be isolated and she was now well enough to be in with other children. She still was not talking or walking, but this room generally was used for infants, and they didn't care.

Moving her bed and furniture was a lot simpler than trying to gather all the possessions which had collected. Worse than gathering her treasures was trying to fit them into the one night stand in the new room. It was obvious that some of the toys had to go home.

Without her help, it was difficult to decide which she wanted to keep with her, and which she wanted saved at home. We eventually narrowed it down and had things pretty well in order. However, each time she regained a skill, someone would find just the right toy or game to help her practice it. Before long, she had taken over the whole corner of the room. The nurses were so interested in anything that would help her (and they were often the donors of the gifts) that they never complained about all the clutter which accumulated.

In mid-January, Ginny's progress picked up again and her balance improved to a point that she could sit in a wheel chair. She tended, however, to list to one side and if she slid down, she could not lift herself back. Diane and I worked one day and devised a sling out of diapers and safety pins that made an effective seat belt. It enabled her to sit up comfortably for lengthy periods . . . and made life much more interesting for her.

We'd frequently have lunch on the porch, listening to records.

(I had brought all her favorites from home—including "Mary Poppins" which, before the accident, she could sing, word for word, both sides. We had hoped that possibly she would try to sing—another straw to grasp for in the search for speech.)

After her breakfast and bath in the morning, the nurses would bring her out into the hall so she could watch all the activity.

The first attempt at "standing" was more difficult than the sitting. It took three of us to support her. Raleigh locked her own arms under Ginny's armpits and around her chest. A student nurse braced her hips and torso. I held her ankles with my hands and stiffened her knees with my shoulders. Her joints seemed to be made of rubber. There was just no strength or control in the muscles for her to help herself in any way. The color drained right out of her face and she began to cry.

The first time was only a split second; the effort was totally exhausting. The next time she lasted a little longer. Each time it became easier and her endurance increased. By mid-January, she was able to use a "standing table"—a wooden frame that supported her from the waist down and gave her a play table on which to rest her elbows for a little added stability.

Raleigh felt that it would do Ginny a lot of good to see some of her brothers and sisters. The therapy department was quite empty on Saturday afternoons. Ginny was scheduled last so that most of the other patients would already be finished. Each Saturday, I brought one or two of the other children over to spend "therapy" with her. She was delighted to see them, and they quickly learned how to play with her.

Celia and Bernadette brought some blocks that we had at home. While Ginny was in the standing table, Celia would make towers for Ginny to knock down. At first, Ginny couldn't move or direct her arm. Celia grasped her wrist and pushed her hand into the stack of blocks. They went clattering to the floor. Ginny laughed and Celia was busy picking them up, to play again. Before many sessions were completed, Ginny was starting to push them down by herself.

Next, Bernadette decided to teach her to build with them. She'd place a block in Ginny's hand, move it to the tower, release it and encourage, "See, Ginny, you can do it!" Both her sisters seemed to have an understanding of exactly what to do to "help Ginny get better."

Raleigh asked me to bring Ginny's shoes from home in order to give her feet a little more support and facilitate standing. Her shoes had been new three days before she was hurt.

The day of the accident, Joseph had picked up the one shoe that was thrown off, brought it home and put it on the hutch in the kitchen. The back was badly crushed. Evidently the truck had rolled over it.

Just as I couldn't throw out the flowers Ginny had picked, I couldn't move her broken shoe. For many days that shoe seemed to symbolize something—but I never knew quite what it was.

The other shoe was packed in the bag with the rest of her clothing that was removed in the emergency room the day of the accident. After it became apparent that she would live, I was then able to take both shoes and put them away in her closet.

Now that Ginny again needed the shoes, I took the broken one to a shoemaker to have it straightened. He knew nothing of the accident. He looked it over and said, "What happened to that? It looks like it was run over by a truck!"

He was preoccupied and didn't hear me say, "It was."

The third week in January we had a heavy snow, and since driving was difficult, the hospital was unusually quiet. Almost no visitors were able to get there.

One of the neurosurgeons, Dr. Ronis, took the opportunity to amuse Ginny by having a wheel-chair race with her down the corridor of the pediatrics ward. A nurse pushed Ginny's wheel chair and Dr. Ronis propelled his, using the handgrips on the wheels. Since the doctor was not used to the chair and the nurse was being cautious pushing Ginny, it was a relatively slow race—but Gin enjoyed every bit of it.

Ginny's spontaneous laugh was one of the few ways that she could clearly indicate that she was aware of what went on around her. Everyone—including Dr. Ronis—took great pleasure in making her laugh. After the wheel-chair race, he took Ginny's little granny cap off her head and put it on his own. He had a forehead that extended almost to the back of his neck. He told Ginny he needed her cap to keep the wind from blowing all his hair around. She caught the joke immediately and laughed.

Even though I had become convinced that Ginny's memory was intact, I still had not been able to get any of the doctors to agree with me. They said it was still too soon to be sure. I took this opportunity to tell Dr. Ronis about something Ginny had done the previous day which made me more certain that her memory was functioning.

Her physical therapy sessions now included some time in a Hubbard Tank. This is an oversized bathtub in which she could float on her back while Raleigh and I held her. The purpose was to get her to kick her legs to regain the back-and-forth movements necessary for walking.

As we worked with Ginny, I remembered the active child she had been the previous summer, spending hours in our backyard swimming pool. I suddenly had a mental picture of her holding on to the side of that pool, leaning back into the water to wash her hair out of her eyes.

Impulsively, I said to her, "Gin, do you remember when you used to swim? Show Raleigh how you got your hair out of your eyes." She rested back on my hand and dipped her head back into the water!

"Thank you again, God."

As I concluded telling this to Dr. Ronis, I said that before the accident Ginny was a good swimmer. He glanced at Ginny, realized she was listening, and corrected me, "Ginny *is* a good swimmer!"

✻✻✻

CHAPTER 10

GINNY WAS ON AN ENTIRELY "SOFT" DIET OF COOKED CEREAL, BABY food, mashed potatoes and ice cream. The firmest food was a thoroughly chopped soft-boiled egg. There was no need for her to chew; everything could be swallowed readily.

For a treat, we'd give her lollipops. She still had practically no use of her arms, so we'd hold the lollipop in her mouth and it would just melt on her tongue.

One evening toward the end of January, Dan was feeding her one. She bit down on it, and broke half of it off. I was thoroughly scared—afraid that she would choke.

"Ginny! Either spit it out or chew it up!"

She started grinding away. It sounded like rocks in a cement mixer. She swallowed, took another chunk, and ground that one, too. Before long, she was proud of the empty stick.

When we told the nurses, they were thrilled. "If she can chew lollipops, why is she still on a soft diet?"

In two days she was eating steak!

Eating became a great pleasure for her. She could not walk or talk—but she could eat—and that she did very well. She liked anything and consumed everything that was on the tray. All she needed was someone to feed her. Now she started to gain back all the weight she had lost.

Finally, we had everyone convinced that she still had her memory and understanding. Even without words, she was starting to express her feelings and emotions. Dr. Metcalf, our family physician, visited her every day. She loved him, and let him know it.

A stranger she could "turn off" and completely ignore. She could separate the people who pitied her from the ones that sincerely wanted to help, and she would not respond to those who felt sorry for her.

She loved all the nurses who took care of her, but the technician with the "blood-test kit" who took weekly samples, she out-and-out disliked!

During the early part of January, Ginny had started receiving speech therapy three times a week. The therapist was a tall young man by the name of Frank Volz, and when I first met him I thought he looked more like a professional basketball player than the "speech pathologist" which was his official title.

Of all the people who treated her, I think he exhibited the most patience. He had tested her and felt there was a good chance she could relearn to talk, but session after session brought no response. She would "answer" by shaking her head "Yes" or "No" and pointing, but she just could not utter a sound.

I had always hoped for a sudden breakthrough—a spontaneous return of full speech—but it never came. It was weeks and weeks before the first unidentifiable noise, then months and months of slowly relearning . . . sound by sound.

Frank explained that when the sounds started to come, the vowels would be easier. It took many more muscles to form a consonant than a vowel. The vocalizing of one "ch," by muscle count, was more difficult than passing a football across the yard.

But Ginny never did follow the normal patterns, and started with the consonants. She was able to say "fun," "one," "gun" but couldn't switch from "fun" to "fin" or "fan." She worked hard, but was often frustrated because she just could not make the sounds she wanted.

When all the accepted speech techniques failed to bring results, Frank devised others. He had tested her with "non-verbal" methods and knew that her memory and understanding were there. Somehow, he was determined to release them and turn those few sounds into real communication. But it was so slow.

A few times people asked why I kept believing Ginny would get well. When I replied that I felt she would recover completely, they would look at me, sometimes with doubt—sometimes with pity. They felt I was deluding myself. How could I believe she would recover? How could I believe, when her insurmountable injuries were so obvious?

It seems that when things are going smoothly, we take God for granted. Everything has to get very bad before we realize that God is good. When the other children walked, it was an accomplishment, but I never realized how truly wonderful it is for a child to walk.

Once in a while one of the other children would come home from school, having gotten in trouble for talking in class. While I recognize that you must learn when to talk—and when not to—still do we ever stop to think how marvelous it is to be able to say one word? The months and months of work, the many attempts and defeats, they can all be necessary just to form a single sound! When the din and blare of life become so intense, when the children are all talking at once, stop to think what this world would be if no child ever laughed or sang.

Before we were married, Dan sent me a card with a quotation from Fra Giovanni. In part, it said, "Life is so generous a giver but we, judging its gifts by their covering, cast them away as ugly or heavy or hard." Now that message had new meaning.

Ginny's accident offered so many gifts. So much that we often overlook now became evident. How quick we are to complain about things that really do not matter . . . the importance we place on "nothings."

She gave courage to other patients in therapy. She was always happy, patient and willing to endure whatever was necessary to help her recovery.

One man disliked everything about his therapy sessions. He resisted and rebelled until the day he met Ginny. From then on he came willingly, and put up with his own treatment, just so he could visit with her. His wife brought a doll for Ginny one day. She wanted to thank Gin for having made her husband's illness a little easier to bear.

Another man was next to Ginny on the "mat," having a particularly painful session. He was sweating—trying not to make a scene in front of her. She rolled over and kissed his hand.

Another patient remarked, "How can I complain when that little girl faces everything she does with such courage!"

And so if you remove the ugly, heavy covering, there were gifts. She gave other patients hope and happiness and strength; her brothers and sisters, love and compassion; and she gave us perspective, understanding, gratitude and a greater faith than we had ever known.

At length, Ginny was beginning to get some controlled motion in her arms—although it was something of a useless combination. The left arm would not move, but that hand could grasp. She could move her right arm, but could not grasp with her right hand. With the back of her right hand, she would rub her eyes constantly and finally came up with the delightful accomplishment of being able to pick at her nose. I was complaining to the therapist that of all the things available for her to relearn, did it have to be that?

Commented Raleigh, "At least, it's great finger movement!"

We kept encouraging her to feed herself. We would hold the spoon in her right hand and fill it for her. If we kept the hand closed around the handle of the spoon, she was able to get it to her mouth. It took weeks, but she loved to eat, and worked away. Finally she began to grasp with the right hand.

This opened whole new fields of exploration. She now had grasp and movement in the right arm. She tried to propel her wheel chair by herself! Of course, doing it one-handed, she could only go around in circles, but it was quite an accomplishment as far as she was concerned—and she was delighted! If we started her off at just the right spot in her room, she could travel in one huge arc and finish up in the hall. She generally wouldn't stop in time and bumped into the wall. Fortunately there was little damage other than some chipped paint. It was counted as more progress. She was able to get herself from her room to the hall. Scratched paint was a small price to pay for such a stride.

Because she was always cheerful, she quickly won the hearts of everyone—particularly the other patients. Children are great in their ability to accept and overlook. Adults would ask, "Why is that little boy in pink pajamas?" The children didn't even seem to notice the overgrown "crew cut." The warmth of her smile mattered more. It really didn't upset them that she couldn't talk; they'd talk for her.

One older boy had his leg in a full cast. He was allowed to ride up and down the hall in his wheel chair. He'd come to "call for her." The nurses would get Ginny all fixed up in her wheel chair, and he'd take her for rides.

Consider the effort he exerted to do it! His leg was rigid and perpendicular to his body—not a particularly comfortable position to start. He'd line up both wheel chairs and propel his with one hand and hers with the other. The only difficulty was, now they both went around in circles. He devised a new system. He would get the chairs straightened out again, move forward as far as he could and still reach back, get the arm of her chair and pull her up alongside—move forward—pull her again!

He became adept and would make it up and down the hall smoothly and freely. Each time things were quiet for her, he'd come down to her room. "Hi, Ginny. Want to go for a ride?"

When he was discharged, she was obviously sad. It was the first time that it was apparent that she missed someone who left.

Another little girl was extremely fond of Ginny and wanted to give her something. Her mother brought a stuffed toy with little bells inside. There was an elastic loop attached to the top of the toy. When jiggled on the elastic, the bells would ring.

Since Ginny's grasp was better with the left hand, she would hold the loop with that hand. It wasn't long before she started to swing that arm a little to make the bells ring. By diligent practice, she was soon able to bounce the toy vigorously. That little girl had wanted to give Ginny something. She helped her regain the use of her left arm!

✻✻✻

CHAPTER 11

BEFORE THE ACCIDENT, IT HAD ALWAYS SEEMED DIFFICULT FOR ME TO get out of the house during the day. Now for almost three months, I had been to the hospital every day—sometimes twice or three times during a day.

Many of the neighbors who "baby-sat" for me had small children of their own, so I would take baby Roberta and Celia (who attended kindergarten in the afternoon) to them. The older children learned the schedule and knew where "home" was each day. I would try to get back before school dismissal, but seldom made it. Ginny would take a short nap after lunch, and when she woke it always seemed the most fruitful time of the day. She was rested, willing to work, and always seemed on the brink of another stride forward.

I would take her for her afternoon therapy session and by working with her at that time, it seemed I often had another "first" to report when I got home.

One afternoon, toward the end of January, I came home just after three o'clock and stopped to pick up the children. They were at the home of one of my friends who had eight children herself. She hung up the phone as I came in the door.

She had been trying to reach me at the hospital. Her face was anguished . . . her eyes overflowing. She had Roberta in her arms —a compress against the baby's left eye. She had just finished feeding the baby and laid her in the carriage, on her tummy, with her head turned just a little to one side.

Her three-year-old had thrown a ball-point pen. It bounced off the wall into the carriage and hit the baby in the eye. The eye was bleeding. She had immediately applied the cold compress and tried to reach me. She was heartbroken . . . inconsolable.

Fortunately, Dr. Metcalf was still in his office. He asked me to bring the baby right over. Dan was not yet home from work, so our oldest son, Paul, only eleven, had to be the "man of the family." He held the baby and I drove the few miles to the doctor's office. As it had been the day of Ginny's accident, in my mind was simply, "Dear God, please. . . ."

Dr. Metcalf looked at it, found the eyeball punctured and immediately called a specialist. He gave me directions and we were on our way again.

The doctor finished his patient and examined Roberta right away. I held the baby while he put a dye into her eye. The color made it apparent that the iris was punctured and the tissue was protruding. It could conceivably heal properly, but he felt it safer if it was "covered." He wanted to operate.

I explained that she had trouble with her heart and gave him the name of the specialist who had been seeing the baby. He decided to postpone the operation till the following day.

He called the hospital. They had a bed. I was to admit her immediately. He put in a medication, bandaged the eye and we left for the hospital.

At the hospital admitting office, the woman at the desk immediately recognized me as "Ginny's mother." Instead of going through the normal routine, filling out forms, she decided to take us right up and get the information later.

Paul was so tall that she never questioned his age and invited him to come along to visit Ginny while I took care of Roberta. She gave me a glance that said if you don't tell me his age—and I don't ask—no one will stop him. After all his help this afternoon, he at least deserved to visit Ginny for a few minutes.

We had never tried to break hospital rules, but I appreciated her wisdom that this was a time when it would be reasonable to bend them a little! I left Roberta with one of the evening nurses, and went with Paul to Ginny's room.

She was pleased with his visit. I told her Roberta had a hurt eye and was in a room down the hall. It was hard to know if she understood at all. Paul stayed to play with her, and I went back to help with the baby.

We changed Roberta into "hospital clothes" and got her settled. The nurses had all become so attached to Ginny, that now they felt Roberta belonged to them too.

I went back to the admitting office and that same thoughtful woman had taken out Ginny's records, copied all the duplicate information and only needed the baby's name and birth date.

Every earlier phone call to Dan had been unanswered. Now he would be home from work. I can't explain how much love and gratitude I felt at that moment because he is the kind of man I could call, without hesitancy, tell him what had happened, and know he would accept it. Thank God we both can remain calm in a crisis. It is much easier to do all that you must when called upon.

By the time Paul and I arrived home, the other children had all been fed supper and returned home.

I went to my friend. The deepest hurt for me was the grief it brought to her. It was such a freak accident, there was no explaining it. But, if it had to be, why couldn't one of my own children have thrown the pen—or why couldn't it have happened at home? It saddened me that we were entwining others into such deep heartache.

I tried to reassure her that everything would be all right. I'm sure she knew I felt no ill will toward her little boy—and hoped and prayed that she didn't blame him. But, there was no way I could console her. She was heartbroken. This was one of those times when I felt a heavy responsibility to say the right thing—to do the right thing—and was so completely inadequate.

When we returned to the hospital that evening, Dan took Ginny in her wheel chair to visit, but because Roberta was isolated, she could come only to the door. I held Roberta so she could see her. She seemed unhappy that she couldn't hold the baby. But, at least, she seemed to know Roberta. I had often wondered if she even remembered the baby, only seven weeks old at the time of Ginny's accident. Ginny had now been in the hospital for over three months. She had been away from home longer than she had lived with Roberta. In the midst of our concern for the baby, it was encouraging that there was yet another sign of Ginny's memory.

The operation was scheduled for the following afternoon. Ginny was napping as the time approached for Roberta's operation, so I dressed the baby in her "gown" and then walked with her till it was time to go. I wasn't afraid of the actual surgery—but her weak heart terrified me. Could she withstand the anesthesia? I was deeply afraid that I was holding her for the last time.

Ordinarily, a mother is asked to leave before a child is wheeled out for an operation. Possibly the nurses sensed my apprehension. I appreciated their letting me have those last few minutes with her. Again I walked and prayed, "Dear God, please. . . ."

They came for her and I watched as they wheeled her down the hall, past the doors, around the corner . . .

It was time for Ginny's afternoon therapy session—and again it was better to keep busy. I dressed her and took her downstairs, but my heart wasn't in it. I kept watching the clock, trying to guess how long it would take. I didn't want to go back to Roberta's empty bed, but was anxious to know.

The secretary in the therapy department came over and told me pediatrics had called and Roberta was back from the operating room. I thoughtlessly didn't explain to Ginny that it meant everything was all right—she had lived through the operation. In my anxiety, I ran right up to the baby's room.

The therapist told me later that after I left, Ginny stopped exercising. They finally gave up and brought her back upstairs. While it interrupted a therapy session, they felt it was another indication of her awareness of everything that was going on around her. As they pushed her wheel chair through the doors of the pediatric ward, by waving her left arm toward the baby's room, and nodding her head, Ginny stopped them at Roberta's door. She wanted to check on the baby herself.

Roberta was still under the effects of the anesthesia—and resting peacefully. "Dear God, thank you." I don't know who was more relieved, the doctor or I. Later I learned that he, too, had been concerned; he was confident that he could operate successfully . . . but could she live through it?

Everything was going well, and although Roberta was in an oxygen tent most of the time, she was allowed out to be fed. We would bring Ginny in her wheel chair to Roberta's door and a nurse would feed one while I fed the other, so they could eat together.

Ginny enjoyed "having lunch out" and my earlier doubts about her memory of the baby were quickly dispelled. That was *her* baby sister; there was no question about it.

Occasionally one of the nurses would tease Gin, "Roberta is such a nice baby. Can I take her home with me? You have lots of sisters; couldn't I have just this one?"

Ginny's brow would furrow, her eyes darken; her head would shake an emphatic "No!" Roberta was "her baby." The nurses could take care of her while she was hurt, but Gin made it very clear, she wasn't giving away Roberta—or any of her sisters, for that matter.

One day as I was leaving Roberta's room, Dr. Stivelman was in the hall. (He was the doctor who lived near the scene of Ginny's accident. Although he was not on Ginny's case, he looked in on her whenever he could. He had just been told about Roberta.) He came over to me, put his arm around my shoulder, and asked, "Haven't you people had enough?" He seemed unusually concerned. Later I learned that his own grandson had lost an eye in a similar accident and this must have reopened the wound in his heart!

No matter how tragic a situation, little comical incidents always crop up. It seems the ability to enjoy the comedy helps one face the tragedy.

A new volunteer was sent to help in pediatrics. She was checking the records and remarked "how unusual it was they had two little girls from the same address. They must live in an apartment house. Oh! They have the same last name. They're sisters! Oh, my heavens!"

A few days later, another incident, not comical, but chilling, made us realize how hopeless Ginny's injuries had been. Dan was trying to keep all our medical bills in order. We could not meet these obligations immediately, but he wanted to keep the records straight; we would pay the bills as we were able.

A bill arrived from a medical group because one of the doctors had assisted at Roberta's operation. On the billhead Dan recognized the name of another doctor who, he was quite sure, had assisted at Ginny's surgery the day she had been hit. He had no bill in his file for the work done on Gin.

He called the medical group and explained the situation. A bookkeeper checked the records, came back to the phone and said, "The doctor did assist at Ginny's operation that day but he instructed us not to send a bill inasmuch as Virginia died."

Dan was thunderstruck! He realized that the doctor must have left the operating room convinced that Gin could not survive and had told the bookkeeper not to send us a bill.

"Ginny is alive," Dan explained, "and we believe she is recovering quite well. Please tell the doctor to send us his bill and we'll pay it as soon as we can."

The bill never came.

Roberta's eye healed well. After twelve days in the hospital, she could come home. At that point the doctor could not promise anything, but he was hopeful that it would not affect her vision.

Despite all their efforts and professional proficiency, the nurses had not been too successful feeding her. It was probably a negative kind of satisfaction, but it did make me feel more competent. Feeding her always took hours and I never could coax much into her. If the nurses could do no better, maybe I was doing all that could be done!

* * *

CHAPTER 12

GINNY CONTINUED TO IMPROVE SLOWLY. SHE HAD GAINED BACK ALL THE lost weight, and more, so that the nurses were afraid of my lifting her alone. But instead of its being more difficult because of the increased weight, it was easier because of a new accomplishment. She could now put her arms around my neck and hold on—and how good it was! It was really easier than when I was lifting limp, lifeless weight.

She was now in and out of her wheel chair so frequently that it was left at the foot of her bed, instead of being stored down the hall.

Dr. Noto, the doctor who had done the gastrostomy operation on her stomach, was fond of her and visited whenever he was in pediatrics. One day he had a very sick infant in the bed next to Gin. In rushing from the room to make a phone call, he tripped over her wheel chair. He didn't actually fall but stumbled and made quite a clatter before he recovered his balance. Ginny laughed. Nothing had been said. She *saw* the slapstick humor in the whole situation and without recognizing the seriousness of the infant's plight, or the urgency of the phone call, she thought the doctor's discomfiture quite comical.

Already out in the hall, Dr. Noto was so intent on what he was doing that he had not heard her laugh. Later, I told him the story. I was a little apprehensive, not knowing if he would be offended by her amusement at his loss of dignity.

He was pleased. He was so glad to have proof of her vision, awareness of her surroundings, and obvious sense of humor.

He met Dan a few days later and went out of his way to discuss the incident with him, including all the aspects that helped prove her progress. After that, he would frequently greet her with "Have you got a smile for me, or do I have to break a leg?"

Some weeks later, when she could utter only a few sounds, she spotted him in the hall and spontaneously called "Noto." He was gone before I could reach him. She loved him enough that it triggered that tiny breakthrough—if only for a single word. She wasn't able to repeat his name again. I coaxed and coached to no avail. I knew she had said it, but I just couldn't get her to say it again to prove it to anyone else. Her vocabulary was still restricted to just a few sounds.

I am convinced that a tragedy such as Ginny's accident invariably results in a greater good. It profoundly influenced many people and deeply affected their lives. I'm sure, too, that there were many benefits that never came to my attention. But those I heard about gave me renewed faith that she was undergoing all this to help others.

It may be stretching the imagination to include one incident (and I'm sure that it would never be accepted medically), but I like to believe that she had a hand in it.

Occasionally the pediatric ward was empty. Most of the patients had gone home and new ones not yet admitted to fill empty beds. One particular day, Dr. Rosenzweig was the only doctor in the ward. Ginny was his one patient there at that time and he had come into the ward only because he had to visit her. If it had not been for Ginny's accident, there would have been no doctor on the floor at that particular moment.

Down the hall, a little boy had a severe penicillin reaction. Dr. Rosenzweig was with him in a split second and saved his life! Possibly a nurse could have done the same thing, or another doctor called in time, but I like to believe that Ginny had a share in giving that little boy another chance to live.

Possibly, he too was spared for greater things!

I could never bring myself to believe that coincidence is a valid explanation for many of the wonderful experiences of daily life which, in my opinion, can be ascribed only to the direct action of the guiding hand of God.

The greater part of the time, Ginny was most affectionate and cheerful. The only thing she really fussed about was the "stretching" exercises in therapy. This stretching was necessary to keep her leg tendons limber enough so that she would be able—someday—to sit, stand, walk and possibly even run. When they are not being used normally, tendons gradually shrink and tighten, distorting joints, and finally leaving the limbs useless. If there was any chance of her total recovery, it was absolutely necessary that all these tendons be stretched every day.

There were several ways of effecting it, but one method is simpler to explain, enabling one to appreciate how painful it must have been. She would sit with her legs straight in front of her. I would hold her knees down against the mat. Raleigh would kneel in back of her and gradually press forward on Ginny's shoulders till her torso made less than a 90-degree angle with her legs. This would be painful enough if she were feeling well, but under the circumstances it must have been excruciating. Raleigh would get it over with as quickly as possible, but it was still heartbreaking for all of us to see her in pain. The only thing that made it endurable was the knowledge that, without it, her little body would soon be wrung into a helpless knot.

One day Raleigh started to press forward on her shoulders. Ginny was crying. Then suddenly she stopped and looked toward me with all the supplication one could possibly put into a child's face and for the first time cried . . . "Mom!"

I gathered her in my arms, tears streaming down my face. It ended the session for the day, but Raleigh was too choked up to continue anyway!

Just as she couldn't repeat it when she had called "Noto," it was many weeks before there was anything that in any way again resembled "Mom."

At home, whenever there was anything distasteful that had to be done, the children were always counseled to "offer it up." All sorts of sacrifices were offered for Ginny's recovery. Homework was done "that someday Ginny will be able to write." Garbage was carried out "that she will walk." Dishes were washed "that she might regain the use of her hands."

Occasionally the intent was there, but the difficulty of the sacrifice was rather doubtful. When Ginny couldn't eat, the children had cleaned plates of food they didn't like "so that someday she would be able to swallow." Once, five-year-old Celia proudly announced, "I really don't like this ice cream, but I'll have another big plate so I can offer it up for Ginny."

When the "stretching" was so painful for Ginny, I'd try to get philosophical with her and remind her about the other children offering sacrifices for her. She knew, from before the accident, how anything difficult could be offered as a prayer. Somehow, it always seemed so much more worthwhile if it was offered for someone else.

From being in the hospital, she knew others who were very sick. All her friends in therapy—people crippled by strokes, amputees, muscular dystrophy victims—they all needed extra prayers. It hurt when she was stretched, but crying didn't make it hurt any less, and it only made Raleigh feel bad. If she would go through with the stretching—and not cry—and offer it up—maybe it could help someone else get better.

Sometimes it helped her and she could hold back the tears throughout the whole session. How sweet those sacrifices must have been, when a little child who was so sick could endure her own pain and offer it for someone else!

It wasn't always easy, however, for her to be noble. She was also becoming aware enough to evaluate the effect of her crying. Raleigh was tenderhearted; Ginny knew it. If she cried hard enough, Raleigh would stop as soon as the absolute minimum had been reached. Ginny even went so far as to try crying *before* Raleigh had started—probably hoping for a complete reprieve!

Dan frequently stopped to see her on his way home from work. Ahead of his usual schedule, he arrived one day while she was still at therapy. Just as he came in the door, before Raleigh even touched her, she started to cry as hard as she could.

He is easygoing with the children, but if things get too far out of hand, his word is law. They all know that when he is stern—he means it!

Dan recognized that Raleigh hadn't started, and that Gin was simply putting on all the fuss to avoid the stretching. He looked at her with all the severity he could muster under the circumstances and told her to cut it out or she would get a good spanking!

She turned off the noise and studied him, wondering if he really meant it. She must have decided that he did. Exercises were completed without any more nonsense.

Which probably proves that, in dealing with children (as in many experiences of life), idealistic philosophy should be tempered with sound practicality.

Afterward, Dan and I were talking to Raleigh about the incident. On the face of it, it seemed that Ginny was simply getting "bratty." But, it was a significant step forward in her recovery. She had progressed to a point where she needed discipline!

Nurses on the floor soon became aware of the same need. Even though everyone loved her and had the deepest sympathy because they knew all she had been through, it was becoming more and more obvious that she was getting "spoiled." She was everyone's pet. She could get all the attention she wanted. She knew it, and was starting to play it to the limit.

One evening when we came to visit, one of the nurses called me aside. She seemed reluctant to talk, but felt she had to tell me. She had tried to put Ginny in for a nap after the afternoon therapy session. (Ginny fatigued readily and really needed the extra sleep.) She had gotten her all changed and settled and told her to put her head down and go to sleep. Ginny screamed at her and tried to hit her. The nurse gave her a good swat, told her to go to sleep, and walked out of the room!

She told us she was sorry and hoped we wouldn't be angry but felt it was necessary. Ginny would be going home someday and she did not want to send her back so spoiled that she would be uncontrollable.

I was pleased that she loved Ginny enough that she was concerned for the "whole child." It would have been much easier if she had just given in to her. I appreciated her interest in Ginny's (and my) future!

It was good of the nurses to be open with me. Many times, I'm sure it was difficult for them to tell me, for fear of repercussions, but I respected their honesty. Anyway, they generally did what I would have done had I been in their place.

The whole pediatric ward generally emptied out on weekends. Most children are in the hospital for only a few days, and their confinement was usually scheduled so they would be back home with their families by Saturday. It meant that the weekends were quiet, and Ginny was frequently alone in her room for the two days.

One Saturday, when Ginny was all alone, one of the nurses came into the room to make up the emptied beds, partly because it needed to be done, partly just to keep her company.

Since Ginny still could not talk, she couldn't hold a conversation, but it created activity for her to watch, and she was well aware of having the company.

The nurse started to lower the side on a crib. It slipped out of her grasp and smashed her finger most painfully. She expressed her reaction to the situation with a word that wasn't quite the best choice in the presence of a six-year-old, though a most natural reaction to the situation.

She told me about the incident because she was afraid that Ginny had heard her even though she was in the opposite corner of the room. She was ashamed of what had happened and concluded most apprehensively, "She hasn't started to talk, but if that is the first word she says, I'll die!"

To date, she hasn't used it.

***

CHAPTER 13

EARLY IN FEBRUARY, THE DOCTORS BEGAN TO DISCUSS THE POSSIBILITY of Ginny's coming home. Although her nursing care was primarily custodial, she still needed the eleven therapy sessions every week.

It was agreed that I was capable of the "nursing" she would need, although Dr. Metcalf, knowing all else I had at home, did not think it wise to make the change at that time. Besides, he felt it would have been impossible to bring her back to the hospital twice a day for therapy.

I thought the whole idea had been shelved, when Raleigh suggested another possibility. Ginny had been in the hospital for three and a half months. She wasn't accustomed to being with the family. They might not be ready for her. Raleigh had some serious questions about her readjustment to family life, and the effect it would have on her.

She spoke to Dr. Rosenzweig and they agreed to try an experiment. Ginny was given a "pass" for the following Sunday. She was allowed to go home for a six-hour visit. We signed a release taking full responsibility for her care, health and well-being. It was no more than our normal responsibilities as parents, but it was somewhat frightening to see it in writing.

Saturday evening, when we left her at the close of visiting hours, we explained that we would be there just before lunch the following day. We would bring clothing to get her all dressed and she could come home and have dinner with us.

She could nod "Yes" or "No," so she helped plan the menu. By a long process of elimination, we found out that she would like Dan to cook steak outside. She always insisted that "Daddy was the best cook," and was most enthusiastic about deciding on the meal.

In the morning, the children were all wound up with excitement. After everyone went to Mass, Dan and I left to get her.

We were to be there at eleven o'clock and arrived promptly. Diane said that Ginny was wide-awake when she came on duty at seven that morning. Evidently the idea of 11 A.M. wasn't too clear to Ginny, and she wanted to be up and ready. She had wanted no part of breakfast, and had no use for pajamas after her bath. She just wanted to go home. When we arrived, she couldn't get into her "going-home" clothes fast enough.

There was always a great joy when we brought a new baby home from the hospital, but it in no way compared to the joy of bringing home the child whose life was given to us twice!

The other children had all been watching for the car and, even though it was freezing, all ran out to meet her. They were all talking at once—each had dozens of questions that had to be asked.

Dan carried her into the house. In the center of the table was a little basket of yellow roses—a perfect "little-girl bouquet." The card read, "Dear Virginia, what happiness you've brought your family today."

That morning at Mass, my mother had met one of her friends and told her the wonderful news that now, almost four months after the accident, Ginny was coming home for a visit! Even though the weather was so cold, that friend made the trip to the florist to send the flowers.

The hospital had loaned us a wheel chair, which the boys brought from the car. The children all took turns pushing her around the house, showing her everything, reawakening all the memories.

Of all the children, somehow Bernadette was always closest to Ginny and seemed to have the greatest understanding of her capabilities and limitations. She realized that all the confusion at once was too much for Gin and convinced the other children that they should leave the two of them alone. She set up a little table in front of the wheel chair and laid out a coloring book and crayons. She held a crayon in Ginny's hand and helped her to color. Her awareness of Ginny's problems was remarkable in a child only seven years old.

It was good to have Ginny at the dinner table again—even if she was in a wheel chair instead of sitting on the long bench with all the other little girls. She still needed a great deal of help feeding herself, and was tiring rapidly.

We finished eating and Dan carried her upstairs and laid her in her own bed. She was exhausted and dropped right off to sleep. Seeing her curled up, sleeping so peacefully, it was hard to realize so much had happened.

She had been sleeping in a bed with sides in the hospital, making us reluctant to leave her alone now. Dan brought in a rocker and the Sunday papers and spent the most relaxed Sunday afternoon in many months.

When she awoke, he carried her all around upstairs. She checked it all thoroughly, room by room. Satisfied that so much was the same, yet noticing little things that were different, she was pleased with the tour.

Many of the neighbors and their children had wanted to visit her. It made a full and exciting day. She seemed to recognize all of them and was happy to have their company. Whether the visit was as pleasant for the company is hard to determine. Most of the older children knew what to expect or were wise enough to express their opinions after they left. Some of the younger ones did not seem to understand, but were glad to see her anyway.

The day went too quickly, and we had promised she would be returned by five o'clock. Before we brought her home, we had made a point of explaining to her that she would go back to the hospital for supper. It was just a visit; after a few hours she would have to return. For all the efforts of preparing her, I still had some doubts about telling her it was time to go. (At that point we had permission for only one visit; we couldn't even promise that she could come home again.)

It was getting so near the time that I couldn't put it off any longer. There was no way of avoiding it. Without further preparation, Dan said, "It's time to go back to the hospital, Ginny. I'll get your coat."

I had mentally braced myself for a flood of tears. Instead, she was delighted to go. She really seemed glad to be getting away from home. It broke my heart. I kept telling myself that it really was better than if she had rebelled at going back. Raleigh's anticipation that it would be difficult for her to return home had proved true. I had expected too much and was disappointed. The confusion and excitement had been too great and she seemed anxious to get back to the relative peace and order of the hospital.

Arriving there, she went upstairs eagerly, had her supper with the nurses and still was quite content when we visited in the evening. I expected some emotional response to having been home, but she didn't even balk at our leaving at the end of visiting hours.

The next morning, however, things were different. The sunny disposition was gone. Her spirits were at the lowest ebb the nurses had ever observed. After some deliberation, they decided that she was just seriously homesick. This was the sign that Dr. Rosenzweig was watching for. He granted permission to bring her home every Sunday!

It was now much easier for Ginny and me. I would help her count off the days on her fingers until the next Sunday. We both had something to look forward to.

***

CHAPTER 14

EVEN WITH THE VISITS HOME, THERE WERE STILL SIX AND THREE-QUARTER days every week for Ginny to spend working on recovery at the hospital. During the early weeks of March, she gained a remarkable ability. She was able to hold a pencil. (It is interesting how one's perspective changes under different situations. When a normal child begins to hold a pencil, it seems just natural development. When Ginny could suddenly hold a pencil, it was a noteworthy improvement.) In her first efforts, she held it with her whole fist, the point extending from the pinky side of her hand. She would stab at the paper. The only things she could draw were huge pictures of snowstorms.

After several days of this, Ginny was suddenly able to get a sweeping motion—then a line—then gleeful scribblings—beautiful lines swinging back and forth across the paper.

Then, even better than the "writing," she accomplished something else. When the paper was full, she picked it up between two fingers and turned it over! Such control over the two fingers was heartening to watch.

Having achieved grasp in the two fingers, she was soon holding the pencil properly. Invariably, she would pick up the pencil upside down and the "fine finger movement" that it took to turn it around was magnificent. Typical of a small child, she generally had her tongue curling out the corner of her mouth during the operation. It took such intense concentration and effort to turn the pencil that it was surprising she didn't bite her tongue.

One of Dan's brothers and his wife found a special present for Ginny. They brought her a drawing set containing blank pages.

When a stylus was rubbed over the entire page, a picture appeared. She was delighted and worked with it for hours on end. It gave her the feeling of accomplishment. She could draw a picture. She could do something all by herself.

Through the early months, Ginny had either been alone in a room or with infants. Now older children were being put in with her.

The first girl brought into the room had been hit in the eye with a snowball and it was necessary to keep both eyes bandaged until it rested and healed. She was a pretty little blonde, just a few years older than Ginny. They became the best of friends. She couldn't see and Ginny couldn't talk, but they learned to help each other.

While it wasn't too clear, Ginny could now vocalize enough to convey "Yes" or "No" and the new friend quickly caught on to it. She'd ask questions while Ginny would look around and give the answers. As long as the questions could be answered with a simple "Yes" or "No" they could "converse."

The following day another little girl, a year younger than Ginny, was admitted. She needed surgery to remove a cyst from her knee. She was a bright little imp, and the three of them had a "ball." It was good to see Gin respond so well to the other children and the friendship they gave her.

The second girl's mother had worked with the handicapped and found fat crayons that she felt would be easier for Ginny to grasp. It took hours of practice and patience, but she liked working with Ginny and she enjoyed the rewards of Ginny's slightest advance, just as we did.

After about a week, her daughter's leg had healed and she was ready to go home. Having received the news, she should have been happy. Unfortunately, both she and her daughter had become so attached to Gin that they left in tears, with Ginny crying in her room.

When the first girl's eye healed and it was time for her to leave, Ginny was taken out to the porch, which made the moment a little easier. But there was still a lot of explaining to do when Ginny found the bed empty. However, both mothers promised they would bring the girls to visit us when Ginny was home.

The second Sunday that Ginny came home was much easier on her than the first, though there was more company. The first week only the close neighbors had come. The second week it seemed everyone dropped in. I should have expected it and prepared something to feed them. But I wasn't that foresighted.

Dan's sister and her family stopped in; fortunately she brought a box of candy. We entertained over forty guests on a pound of candy and several pots of coffee. But no one had come to be entertained. They all just wanted to see Ginny—to see for themselves this child who was living proof of God's goodness, as expressed through the wonders of medical science.

Everyone wanted to share in the miracle. Ginny thrived on the attention and improved, if not rapidly, at least constantly!

Bernadette was still closest to Ginny. She was in her glory having Ginny to play with, if only for a few hours. They would sit on the floor, coloring. Gin's grip was so tight the crayons would frequently break. Dettie would never criticize, just help and encourage.

Ginny had great difficulty in relearning to crawl. The left arm gave her more trouble than anything else, and with its unpredictable weakness she often collapsed onto that shoulder. Rather than try crawling when she was home, she would take the easier method of sliding around on her bottom.

Bernadette, however, knew it was important for her to crawl again, and would practice with her, encouraging her and coaxing her to "try once more." Her patience was endless—and heartening to watch.

They would build blocks. Dettie would steady Ginny's hand, helping her to pile them up. When Gin tried by herself, they would generally topple, and Bernadette would simply start again.

They worked on jigsaw puzzles with large pieces. When Ginny was finally able to put one piece in position, all by herself, it was hard to determine which girl was more pleased.

The "police lady" who had crossed Ginny at school always inquired about her progress. One Sunday she stopped to visit. She was out of uniform, but Ginny obviously recognized her, even though she had known her such a short time and hadn't seen her for over four months.

She questioned, "Ginny, do you remember when you used to push the crosswalk button to help me?"

Ginny nodded. Another proof that the time before the accident was not lost from her memory.

Before leaving she asked Ginny to promise that someday she would come back to school and help her again. Ginny's enthusiasm reinforced my belief that some day she would.

For many months before the accident, Ginny had watched the movie schedule in the daily paper to see if *Sound of Music* was playing near us. I had promised when it was nearby, we would go. Now it was playing in the next town, but she was in the hospital.

I wondered about the possibility of taking the whole family to the movies for one of Ginny's "Sunday visits." The doctors and nurses thought it would do her a lot of good and the risks were far outweighed by the advantages it might bring.

In order to avoid a long line at the box office, we wanted to make advance arrangements but unfortunately the theater wasn't able to reserve tickets. We got the children ready, picked Gin up at the hospital, and went to the movies. It must have been quite a sight. Even though we arrived early to avoid the crowd, just our family made a long line, all the children—and Ginny in her wheel chair.

We got everyone settled, with Ginny on the aisle, and Dan right next to her. If she was restless he could take her out without disrupting the whole row of children.

The nicest thing about taking children to a show is watching their reaction and enjoyment. Our children go to few movies, and their appreciation is all the greater. They were enchanted.

However, *The Sound of Music* is long, and Dan noticed that Ginny had lost interest in the screen and was turning to look all around. He wondered if we had overestimated her endurance, if we had made a mistake in trying to bring her. Then he noticed all the children were looking around. The story was getting too sentimental for the kids and they had discovered that if you watch the light coming out of the projection booth, you can try to guess how the picture is changing on the screen!

The whole adventure was a success and after that, any time the music was played on her radio or on the TV in the hospital room, she immediately recognized it.

There had been some apprehension, particularly on the part of the doctors, that she would be exposed to too many germs at the theater, and there was a real risk of her catching a cold. The following morning, her temperature was up. I kept thinking about that paper I had signed "assuming all responsibility for her physical wellbeing" and wondered if she had caught something while we had her out, whether they would cancel any future passes.

But the next day everything was back to normal. Nothing was said, so Ginny and I started counting the days till the following Sunday.

***

CHAPTER 15

Ginny had a way of making friends with parents of other patients. The Lundgren baby who was so seriously ill when Dr. Noto fell over her wheel chair remained in the hospital for a long time. His crib was right next to Ginny's. His parents came every evening. Since it is rather difficult to "entertain" a very sick month-old baby, while his mother was rocking him his father would play with Ginny.

They built a deep, enduring friendship. She would await his visit in the evening as anxiously as ours. She quickly learned which pocket held a "treat" and the two of them would clown together for everyone's amusement.

Even after their baby was well enough to be taken home, they made several trips back to the hospital to visit her.

Right across the hall from Ginny, visible from her bed, was a new infant who had been born prematurely, with multiple complications. The baby's mother was so ill after the delivery that she could not be moved from her room. The father came alone every night. Since the infant was in an incubator, there was little he could do but stand and watch.

Ginny filled a need. He would come over and talk to her, discussing his son's and her progress. From her bed he could watch his son, be near him, yet have something to do. He would take her for walks in her wheel chair. On Valentine Day, he brought her a little satin heart, filled with candy.

For months, Ginny had been spending most of her time in pajamas. Now that she was getting dressed to go home on weekends,

Diane thought it would be good for her morale if I brought slacks and shirts to the hospital. Each morning, after her bath, instead of getting back into pajamas, they would dress her. Diane felt it would be more pleasant for her, and another step toward readjustment to normal life.

She was still wearing diapers, and had grown a bit, more a rounding out of the torso, and a building up of her shoulders. The clothes she had worn before would not fit.

I found two new outfits for her. Being the third daughter, she had been raised on hand-me-downs and was thrilled with the new clothes. Each morning the nurses would let her select what she wanted to wear that day, and each evening I'd accumulate all the dirty clothes and take them home for the wash, so they wouldn't get lost in the hospital laundry. I had been doing her pajamas all along, but there was something nice about sorting clothes at home and again having a stack for Ginny.

At naptime, one day, Diane changed her, hung her slacks over the foot of the bed and tucked her in to rest. Ginny rebelled. Diane scolded her and told her she had to sleep. Ginny put her head down on the pillow, closed her eyes and "played possum." As soon as Diane was out of the room, she pulled herself up on the side of the bed and hauled herself bar by bar down toward the foot of the crib. She reached the slacks and started dressing herself.

Diane tiptoed back to see if she had gone to sleep. Ginny was sitting up in bed with the slacks pulled on—almost up to her waist!

Ginny won that round with the nap—but the story spread quickly. From then on, all the nurses insisted that she help in dressing herself!

Whenever she could get away, Sister Agnes stopped over to visit Ginny. One evening she arrived just as the supper trays were sent up. Ginny was beginning to be able to feed herself a little, but still needed a lot of help.

The head nurse was shorthanded that evening. Other patients needed help and there was no one available to feed Gin. Since several of her own children went to St. Christopher's, she knew Sister. She analyzed the whole situation and reached the only practical conclusion.

Sister Agnes rolled up her sleeves and fed Gin. (It was necessary to roll up her sleeves, since Ginny's enthusiasm and spasticity were not always conducive to the neatest table tactics.)

It seemed a practical and needed example of "feeding the hungry."

It was generally more convenient, or necessary, to give the patients bed baths, so the tub in the "girls' bathroom" was seldom used. Diane, nevertheless, came with a gift for Ginny—bubble bath. One quiet morning she filled the tub with warm water and overflowing bubbles, and went to all the trouble of moving Ginny in a wheel chair and lifting her into the tub. It would have been quicker and easier just to have given her the regular bed bath. But the nurses were never concerned about what was "easier." A bubble bath would be fun for Ginny (and in all honesty, for Diane too); it would be a break in the hospital routine. As long as no one else was neglected, if things could be done, why not?

I'm sure it was this attitude on the part of all the nurses—to make the effort to do the little "extras"—that helped her recovery immensely.

Ginny had no more control than a little infant, so for months she wore diapers. But as more healing took place, this became another field that had to be conquered.

If you try to train a baby before it can talk and "tell you," before there is any real understanding, it is practically impossible to do more than train yourself to be there at the right time. With Ginny the situation was slightly different. She knew what we were talking about; she understood what she was supposed to do. She just could not tell us when she had to go. More difficult, she couldn't get out of bed, or even propel herself well enough to get assistance when she needed it.

We started having some success with putting her on a bedpan regularly. Then we progressed to taking her to the bathroom whenever it was practical. It was all working very well, as long as someone remembered at the right times. She was pleased to be out of the diapers and proud to have everyone praise her for being such a good girl, going to the bathroom.

Just taking her frequently was not the answer. Some system had to be devised so that she could tell us when it was necessary. Otherwise, she would spend most of every day on the john. We tried giving her a little bell, explaining that when she "really had to go" she should ring the bell, and someone would come and help her. The outcome of this system should have been predictable. Give any six-year-old girl a bell, and what will she do? Ring it all day long. After many false alarms, we all realized that it just wouldn't work.

Another system—a silent system—was needed. One of the nurses found the solution. One evening when she was caring for Ginny, she had an idea. She made a little sign that said "Bathroom, please" tied it to a ribbon and pinned it to Ginny's shirt.

A large window in the hall wall separated Ginny's bed from the nurses' station. Now, when she "had to go," all she had to do was knock on the window and hold up the sign.

The first success was unbelievable. When it was urgent, she would let us know, we would take her and the whole program was working to perfection. Soon, however, she gained more control. She thought it great sport to be taken out of bed, plopped in a wheel chair and run down the hall to the "big-girls' room" that also housed the bathroom.

She soon devised her own system. She would watch the desk. If anyone was sitting down, apparently not busy—just filling out charts or doing the endless paperwork—she would knock and wave her "warning flag." It added a little more variety to her life to make the trip down the hall and even six drops she considered a valid indication that she "really had to go!"

***

CHAPTER 16

THE SUNDAY VISITS WERE HAVING A GOOD EFFECT PHYSICALLY AS WELL as mentally. When she was home, she would play on the floor with the other children, crawling and sliding; unconsciously as well as deliberately, practicing and regaining the lost co-ordination. The six-hour visit became one long, pleasant therapy session.

We were willing to let her be as independent as possible. She was on her own, expected to do all she could for herself. She was given help only when she absolutely needed it. She needed support on the stairs, but could pull herself onto the couch. She had to be helped onto a straight chair, but soon learned how to slide off it safely. Her food had to be cut, but she was working hard at feeding herself. It was messy—but the only way she could relearn.

Dr. Holtzman had been observing the results of these visits; evaluating her improvement as well as our handling of Ginny at home.

The doctor evidently felt our management of the situation was satisfactory. If I learned to do all the routine exercises, and would do them twice a day, we could consider the possibility of her coming home permanently. He would let me know when he was confident that I could do the job.

I had been observing Raleigh's technique for the past five months. Whenever possible, she taught me to do the exercises with Ginny. It was now just a case of going over them, to be sure I knew thoroughly what needed to be done.

The major "stretching" exercises were now reduced. Those tendons were in good shape. The most critical problem was in her ankles and feet. The left foot was doing quite well. She had the control to manipulate the foot moderately well. The right foot was a different matter. If she lifted her right leg, the right foot hung down. She had absolutely no ability to pick up that foot or direct the movements of the ankle. It was imperative that tendons in the back of both ankles (but especially the right one) be stretched twice or more every day.

She would lie down, I'd grasp the heel in the palm of my hand, brace the sole of her foot against my arm and press until it forced that foot up to less than a 90-degree angle with her leg. It hurt, but she put up with it.

Other than that, it was simply a case of having her do push-ups and sit-ups to help increase her general muscle tone.

Around the middle of March, Dr. Holtzman sent for me one day and simply said, "It will be all right now if we see Ginny only three times a week."

I didn't fully comprehend what he was telling me, and simply acknowledged it with, "Fine. Thank you." He was on his way to another appointment so I just stood there by myself. The message started to penetrate. He had told me that she could come home! I started back upstairs to tell the nurses who had been caring for her. By the time I got to the pediatric ward, I was half running, half flying! I tore down to the desk.

"Ginny can come home for good!"

Everyone was overjoyed, asking at once, "When?" I hadn't even found out.

Back down to the therapy department. Dr. Holtzman said that it was all right with him, any time I could work out all the details. He simply wanted her brought back for three sessions a week.

I started looking for some of the other doctors to be sure none of them had any restrictions on the homecoming. They all agreed; as long as I brought her for monthly office visits, it was fine. That was Tuesday afternoon. The general consensus was that it could be worked out by the beginning of the following week.

By the time I had driven home to tell Dan the news, I had moved it up in my own mind to the weekend.

Dan was just as thrilled. We talked it over. Roberta had to go to the heart specialist for a check up the next day, Wednesday. Dan asked, "Why not bring her on Thursday?" God bless him! After all his patience for almost five months, he didn't want to wait an extra minute more than we absolutely had to.

Ginny had become part of the hospital routine. Moving her out was going to be more involved than I had anticipated. The first problem we ran into . . . no one was sure which doctor was supposed to discharge her. The day of the accident she had been admitted as Dr. Metcalf's patient. He felt, however, since Dr. Burstein had done the brain surgery, and so much still depended on her head, it was more his responsibility to sign the discharge. Dr. Burstein, though, felt that Dr. Rosenzweig was the pediatrician in charge, responsible for her total care. Therefore, he should sign the release.

I never could figure out why there was such a big concern. I guess that they still had trouble believing that she had lived and was recovering. No one seemed to want to be the last one to put his name on her hospital records. I never found out who did the job. The nurses simply informed me that the permission was granted for her to leave on Thursday.

I hated to take the time on Wednesday to make the hour's drive to the heart specialist, but Roberta's health was important too. The doctor was satisfied with her condition and felt it was not necessary for her to be seen for six months. (I always felt it was progress when we got a six-month postponement on an appointment. When a patient must be seen in two days, I worry.)

The rest of Wednesday afternoon and evening were spent in preparing for Ginny's homecoming. The arrival of a queen would not have caused more excitement.

We brought home as much of Ginny's gear as possible, and she would gladly have gotten into the cartons of toys to come home that night. In cleaning out her night table, it was a pleasure to remove the casts and drop them in the wastebasket. She would need them no longer.

The public relations department wanted to do a story for the hospital newspaper. They also had invited the daily papers to cover the event. In order to give the photographers time, we agreed to make the departure right after lunch.

Dan had to work in the morning. I had to make one more therapy session to learn how to bandage her ankles to give her extra support. We decided that I would go in the morning for therapy, then come home at lunchtime to get Dan.

When I arrived at the hospital, she was sure it was time to go home. She generally loved going to therapy. Today she wanted no

part of it. She still couldn't talk, but she made herself understood
. . . clearly. I had said she was going home this day. She wanted
nothing else, especially going to therapy. She looked at me as if I
had betrayed her.

It took much convincing to make her believe we would go home
after lunch. She went to therapy, under protest! The instruction
was brief. She was too anxious to leave to co-operate with any exercises. I agreed to do them later in the day.

There were many "good-bys" from all her friends, the other patients there, as well as all the staff who had helped make this day
possible.

We went back upstairs so she could have her lunch. She regarded
the meal in the same light as the therapy session. If we skipped it,
we could go home sooner.

Unfortunately, I still had to get Dan and her "going-home"
clothes. Once more, she was heartbroken. I hadn't realized what a
depressing effect these arrangements would have on her. But with
her enthusiasm for leaving, if we were to pick her up at seven in
the morning, she would have been ready to go at 5 A.M.

While she gladly would have gone home in her slacks, I finally
convinced her that I would get a pretty dress and her coat. When
I left, she seemed to have some grave doubts that I was really coming back for her.

We were back in a little while, and her enthusiasm took over
again!

Some of the volunteers and nurses who had the day off came just
to say good-by. Even though the book says that a professional should
not become emotionally attached to a patient, they all loved Ginny
as if she were their own. She had lived (and almost died) with
them. She had been part of them for 143 days. And so, many of
them gave up their day off to be with her the day she was well
enough to go home.

We got her all dressed in a pretty pale blue dress. Diane found
a ribbon to match and put a little bow in her now partly grown hair.
One of the volunteers brought her a little old-fashioned bouquet.

There were photographers and reporters. Pictures were made and
stories for the papers were written. Even though she had been
so anxious to leave, she was basking in the flood of attention.

The unit clerk, true to her unending thoughtfulness, brought a
cake with candles and gave Gin a party. (At the anniversaries of

three and four months in the hospital, we had cakes with candles and Gin had never been able to blow them out. In those last few weeks, she had relearned, and now very happily blew them out.)

Not only had the staff become attached to Ginny, but I had come to love all of them. I was leaving close friends. They had become a part of my life. Each had shared in her recovery. Words were inadequate to express the love and gratitude I felt. How do you say "Thank you for giving our little girl back to us"? At a time like that, how do you say "Good-by"?

Every nurse, aide and volunteer who could be spared from the floor, came down to the door with us. Discharge was from the emergency entrance. She was going out the door through which she had been carried five months before.

Everyone smiled, wished her well, promised to visit and kissed her good-by. Dan wheeled her to the car, lifted her out of the wheel chair and put her in my arms. He returned the chair to the hospital, and all her friends were crying.

⁂

CHAPTER 17

Even though we had brought Ginny home for the past five Sundays, this was different. Our family was whole again. It wouldn't be for just a few hours. The next morning she would be there. There would be no more evenings, checking that everyone was asleep, having to walk past an empty bed. She was ours again.

Mrs. Clancy had taken care of the other children while we were getting Ginny from the hospital. Typical of her kindness, she baked a cake and decorated it "Welcome Home Ginny."

A photographer from one of the papers had not been able to get to the hospital in time. He called and asked if it would be all right if he came to the house. He arrived during dinner, just as we were ready to cut the cake.

With an apology for interrupting the meal, he assured us he'd need only a few minutes. He grouped all the children around the kitchen table, then asked two of them to hold the cake near Ginny so people could tell which child was the celebrity. He didn't realize what a lift he had given us. In the picture it wouldn't be obvious which child had been so severely injured!

We leisurely finished our dessert and coffee. For the first time in over twenty weeks, we didn't bolt down our meal and rush out to be at the hospital in time for visiting hours.

Just as it was good for us to have the family together, life at home was wonderful for her. She was again "one of the kids."

When it was bedtime, once more we were faced with the problem of safe sleeping accommodations for her. When she had been home for the visits, one of us had always stayed in the room with her when she napped. Clearly, it was impractical for one of us to stay up all night.

We decided it was important to let her go back, as much as possible, to a normal life, including sleeping in her own bed. We had thought of improvising sides from parts of a youth bed but decided it would be too "hospitally." Her bed was low, and against a wall. I tucked small pillows under the front edge of the mattress so that she would tend to roll back against the wall and laid thick blankets on the floor alongside, just in case.

Dan and I woke suddenly in the middle of the night. There had been a thud and Ginny was crying. She had fallen out of bed. We picked her up, checked her thoroughly. Nothing was hurt. She soon settled down to sleep again. I was tempted to go back to the plan of making sides, but realized that most of the children occasionally fell out of bed. The possibility that she would get hurt was remote. I had to let her belong.

She slept safely for the remainder of the night, but she probably got much more rest than we did. Even though we had convinced ourselves we were doing the right thing, we were both listening all night. I wondered about the fall. Had she awakened in her own bed, forgotten that anything had ever happened and was simply going to get up to walk to the bathroom?

Friday was completely free, but on Saturday she was to go back to the hospital for therapy. She could not walk unless she had a great deal of support. Dan and I took her without a wheel chair and with one of us on each side of her, holding her up, she "walked" out to the car. Everything was fine until we parked the car at the hospital. She did not want to go in. Somehow she just did not feel sure that if she went in, she would come out again. It was understandable. We had taken her back from those other visits and left her. Could she be sure that this was different?

It took much talking and promising that it was just for therapy. She was going back home as soon as she was through. If you have always kept your word with a child, there is something concrete and reassuring about "you promised." We had promised and she trusted us enough to go.

Some of the nurses knew when she was scheduled and came down to visit her in the therapy department. There was a little teasing about her preference for the hospital. Would she like to come upstairs and stay with them? She couldn't speak, but she could communicate. She made it clear that they were going back upstairs—without her. She was going out that door and back home!

She was willing to do her exercises with Raleigh, but then we ran into a new problem. When Frank Volz did her speech therapy, he always took her to a separate, quiet room, to have her undivided attention. During all the months in the hospital, he generally saw her after her physical therapy. I would work with her physical therapy, but when it came time for speech, I would say good-by and she would go off with Frank, then return to her room for her nap. It was an hour and a half that I could use more productively at home. Since it was the practical way, it had become a routine.

Now she had some doubts again. If she went into that room with him, would we take off while she was gone? I always had in the past months. How could she be sure this was different? He understood what was troubling her and found a quiet corner where she could watch us.

Both therapy sessions were short, but they established the all-important groundwork of convincing her that it was safe to come to the hospital, and that she would be let out again.

As long as I had Dan to help me if I needed him, I wanted to see if I was able to handle her without the nuisance of a wheel chair to load in the car. By putting her coat on while she was seated in the waiting room, getting dressed myself and then getting a good grip under her armpits, I was able to get her up the ramp and into the car. Getting up our back stoop was another question. But I felt that I had to learn to do it. She had to be at the hospital every Tuesday, Thursday and Saturday. I already needed someone to look after the baby while I took her. I had to be able to do it myself or I would need two helpers.

Our back stoop has steep, high steps. It was a little rough, but we made it. Oddly enough, the most difficult part was not the steps but supporting her and opening the door at the same time. Generally, however, we took long enough getting up the steps so that whoever was with the baby spotted us and had the door open before we reached it.

After several therapy sessions, her apprehension wore off and she was willing to go freely and work hard.

It was more beneficial for her to stay at therapy for about two and a half hours. The actual working time wasn't nearly that long, but Raleigh found she could accomplish more by working for a while, then letting her rest. Ginny would do some of the exercises, then play with blocks, string beads or color.

The "playtime" required a lot of help, but hospital volunteers were always glad to have the opportunity to be with her. One did tricks for her and she never tired of his sleight of hand. She soon learned where the dime had vanished and forced him to increase his repertoire. Another worked only on Thursdays. Ginny counted the days on her fingers till she would see him again because it usually meant having a "tea party" in the hospital coffee shop.

Raleigh knew all I had left undone at home. She tried to hurry the sessions to shorten the time I'd spend waiting for Gin. But soon Ginny had enough confidence that I could take her to the hospital and leave her there. She no longer had doubts about my returning. Finally it reached a point where, on my return several hours later, she had difficulty deciding if it was more fun to stay and "play" or return to her brothers and sisters.

Ginny always loved helping at home and now she wasn't going to let the fact that she couldn't walk or talk stand in her way. The second Saturday she was home, Dan found her doing something I wouldn't have believed possible.

In order to clean the floor in his office at home, we always moved all the chairs out in the hall. The floor was done and the wax dry. She took it upon herself to put the chairs back—a job she frequently did before the accident.

When Dan found her, she was busy sliding on the floor, pulling the chairs after her, one by one, until she had them all back in place. The chairs were on casters and there was no way of knowing how many times she rolled them over her fingers. That didn't matter to her, nor did it matter how much effort she had to expend in order to do the job. All that was important to her was the delight and satisfaction to again be "helping Daddy!"

In the early days in the hospital, the doctors would ask her to stick out her tongue in order to determine if she could hear, understand or obey a command. She wouldn't do it. I knew that she was hearing and understanding, and the only reason I could figure out was that she had always thought of sticking out one's tongue as being fresh and bratty.

In working with her speech therapy for months, Frank Volz discovered that she had lost the ability to stick out her tongue. She just was not able to do it. She simply did not have the muscular control required. He tried valiantly to teach her, to no avail. Without that control, it was practically impossible to teach her to speak.

I came to pick her up after a therapy session and Raleigh was elated. "I have to show you something!"

She turned to Ginny. "Stick out your tongue."

Nothing.

Raleigh was crestfallen. She got a tongue depressor and held it in front of Ginny's lips.

"Now, Ginny, push this out of the way with your tongue."

She did it.

It took several more tries, but finally Ginny was able to do it without the depressor. Raleigh had discovered that by giving her something to push against, the muscles got the message. It opened a whole new area of sound that Frank was able to retrain.

Just as there is not one day that a baby starts to talk, there was no way of determining when Ginny's speech came back. It returned over months and months of hard work. But with the new use of her tongue, more of the sounds came together to be words. More of the words were recognizable to others besides ourselves.

Raleigh had worked patiently through seven months. She had kept the range of motion in all her joints; taught her to maintain sitting balance; to roll over and eventually sit herself up. Though it seemed to take forever, because of the greater difficulty with the left arm, she taught her to crawl.

As she did not make a sharp transition from no speech to being able to talk, there was no particular day that she started to walk by herself. She had been working on parallel bars, and she started standing "free." Then there were a few steps. Raleigh tried to get her to use crutches, but Gin refused them. It was difficult to say when she was just stumbling into our arms, and when they were deliberate steps.

Finally, Ginny was able to stand alone for durations of several minutes, and later set a record of thirty-six steps!

Although other therapists worked with Ginny when Raleigh had a day off, I never felt quite as close to them. I loved Raleigh partly because she was such a wonderful person, and partly because she seemed to be the key link between Ginny's lifelessness and recovery.

When Raleigh told me that she would be leaving early in May, I was terribly disappointed—selfishly, because I had doubts that Ginny would work as well with anyone else; more altruistically, because she would not reap the rewards of seeing Ginny walk out of that hospital, a completely recovered, normal little girl.

But I could not be selfish about it. Raleigh was going on to better things. She was expecting her first child and she and her husband were moving back home to Colorado. That baby would be fortunate to have such a mother.

Ginny, too, was close to Raleigh and I was afraid she might not adjust to a new therapist. Rita was to take over her care. I knew Rita from seeing her working in the department. She was very tall, had long dark hair and a deep warm laugh. The few times she had worked with Ginny, I was impressed with her friendliness and competence. I felt sure Rita was capable of doing a good job therapeutically; I just wasn't sure if Ginny was ready for such a drastic change emotionally.

As usual, I had underestimated her. The transition was beautiful and Rita became just as close to Ginny as Raleigh had been.

I often think how fortunate we were to have such loving, dedicated people working with Ginny. Probably, if they weren't loving and dedicated, they wouldn't have chosen that particular line of work for their life profession.

The patience of Frank Volz was finally being rewarded and those sounds were really becoming words. Each day her vocabulary grew just a bit more. It had taken much longer than I expected, and was coming much differently from Frank's earliest predictions, but none of her progress had come the way anyone had expected or predicted. I had always looked for someone to tell me "In two weeks she will do this." Or even, "In five years she will do that." I had always wanted a doctor to know when, or if, she would recover fully. Dr. Holtzman, the head of the therapy department, explained why their answer was always, "We'll just have to wait and see."

In our eyes, things were promising. Ginny was starting to walk and talk. She obviously had her mental faculties. Dr. Holtzman had been in charge of her physical therapy since the earliest days. Dan asked him what her chances were for a full recovery. The doctor answered, "I can't tell you what to expect. I have never seen anyone, injured so severely, who lived." There was no past experience on which to base an educated guess.

***

CHAPTER 18

When I was going to the hospital twice a day, seven days a week, I always thought that there would be more time when Ginny was home. I was now making only six quick trips a week, but the days were as busy as before.

Ginny required a lot of time—helping her up and down stairs, back and forth to the bathroom, buttoning, lacing and tying, and help with relearning everything. The other six children who were in school also needed time—homework to be checked and signed, lunches to be packed, clothing to be pressed and the million things that are important to children had to be listened to and decided upon. The minimum household care, cooking and laundry took time. And, my baby had to have extra time. If there was only some way of getting more hours into those days!

I would get the children out to school in the morning, put dishes in the sink to soak, start a load of laundry and then play "school" with Ginny while I spent an hour coaxing the baby to eat. The "schoolwork" consisted of trying to make "ones" or small "l's" whichever you want to call them, on a straight line. It sounds easy; but often it was a mess—all three facets, the writing, the feeding and the housework.

I'd keep trying to find a more efficient system, but it seldom went smoothly. It was exhausting trying to keep up. Fatigue can make everything seem more difficult. But there was always hope and progress, and it kept me going, working a little harder, trying once more.

Going back to the hospital three times a week for therapy, Ginny made friends with all the other patients there. Most of them were adults, many of them older people. They looked forward to seeing her. She was always in such good spirits that it gave the other patients a lift just to have her smile.

There was a particular fondness between Ginny and an older patient, a frail, wisp of a woman, confined to a wheel chair because she had lost a leg. I never saw anyone so delighted as she, when Ginny could finally call her "Aunt Lil."

One morning in May was unusually raw and rainy as we left for the hospital. Ginny wasn't particularly anxious to go out in the weather. I couldn't blame her. It was such a miserable day, if it weren't for the importance of therapy, I could have been swayed to stay home, too. Trying to build a little enthusiasm for both of us, I talked her into picking a few flowers in the garden. She could take them to someone she loved.

Her tense grip had them pretty well mashed by the time we got there. She didn't even stop to get rid of her coat . . . leading me straight to Aunt Lil. The poor woman filled with tears as Ginny brought them to her. She asked for a paper cup and put them in water.

That evening I met a friend who had visited her mother at the hospital during the afternoon. Her mother's roommate was a sweet old lady known as Aunt Lil. She told my friend, "There's a lovely little girl who comes to therapy. She brought flowers out of her garden to me, on such a wretched day."

By then, the flowers were bedraggled, but there they stood in the little paper cup. Aunt Lil was more pleased with them than if they had been a perfect bouquet!

Just before she left, Raleigh started a treatment that now became a regular routine. The tendons were free enough and Ginny was so active that it was no longer necessary to stretch them. Instead, another difficult and somewhat painful technique took its place.

Her leg muscles were working quite well, except the large one extending down the front of her right leg, from knee to foot. She could not lift her right toes. When she raised her right leg, the foot just hung limp. In walking, she had to lift that foot high enough to clear the toes. It was better than if she had dragged the foot along the floor, but that was about all that could be said for it. One-sided high-stepping had given her an ungainly, uncoordinated gait.

Electrostimulus was started to try to retrain the muscle. It is something of a frightening machine in appearance, covered with dials and outlets. Plugged into this is a long electric wire, connected to a penlike attachment. By touching the weak muscle with this wand, the therapist is able to direct an electric shock at the "lazy muscle." The intensity can gradually be increased until the muscle works involuntarily—thus starting a contact with the brain. The theory was that the electrical contact from the brain to that particular muscle had been broken. If a new channel could be started from the muscle to the brain, use of the foot might be regained.

At first Ginny was apprehensive and fussed a bit. It hurt—just as any electric shock does. How painful it was for her depended on the intensity being used at the time. Starting the session, it was so slight she didn't even feel it. As it was increased, she would wince a bit. When it reached its full impact, the leg muscle would tighten and the foot jerk upward. And Gin would cry.

But it wasn't long till Rita had won her confidence and Ginny would tolerate it stoically. She soon learned how to operate the machine herself and, although she never "operated" on her own leg, she delighted in "treating" anyone within range.

There were countless sessions with it. That area of her leg had been hollow. Now it was starting to fill out. The muscle still wasn't strong enough to lift her foot, but it was obviously better than it had been.

Although it didn't get any less painful for her, Ginny accepted the routine and evidently felt that the end result of being able to walk freely was a worth-while goal.

Before the accident, Ginny was proud of her nickname, "the workin' kid." She wanted to renew the image and didn't consider that her limitations had any bearing on her helping now. Whenever she could, she was right at it. At first, she slid around the living-room floor, picking up toys. Then she learned to walk, holding on to furniture, so that she could dust. She had tried to vacuum from her wheel chair but that didn't work. As she would try to push forward with the wand of the vacuum cleaner, the wheel chair just rolled backward. (She never mastered the use of the brake; she had no intention of staying in the wheel chair, preferring to expend the effort in relearning to walk.)

One morning I left the breakfast dishes and went in to change the baby. Ginny decided to sweep the kitchen floor, a job she always had done willingly. However, she still wasn't too steady on her feet, even when she was holding on to something. The broom hangs in the cellar stairway, at the top of a steep flight, leading down to a rough cement floor. I came into the kitchen. She had opened the door and was standing at the head of the stairs, holding the doorway for support, trying to reach the broom.

Because startling her could completely throw her off balance, I made my way over to her very slowly—reassuring her to just stand still. I would help her get the broom. My heart was in my throat. One slip and we could be right back where we started.

Thank God, her balance was good!

Her reasoning and intelligence were working beautifully, so I told her that she was a good girl for trying to sweep the floor, especially without being asked. (That was a virtue of Ginny's that I have tried in vain to develop in some of my big, strong, capable children.) I explained why it wasn't a good idea for her to try to reach out over the stairs. If she slipped, it could hurt her, badly. She seemed to understand. She may have recognized herself that she was in danger. At any rate, she was satisfied to have me help her away from the open stairway.

She still was much better at crawling, so we substituted a dustpan and brush broom and she did a presentable job. In fact, in her desire to be part of the family, contributing her share, she had done a better job than some of the other children would have done, helping under a "sweep-the-floor-before-you-can-go-out" ultimatum.

Ginny was pleased that she was again able to share the responsibilities of maintaining our home.

***

CHAPTER 19

GINNY HAD BEEN HOME FROM THE HOSPITAL ALMOST TWO MONTHS. While she could walk if she had support, most of the time she crawled or slid on her bottom to get where she wanted to go. Though she wasn't really talking, she could communicate with a combination of the few words she was able to say and her own method of sign language. And, as any six-year-old, there were times when she made up her mind to do something, without asking first if it was a good idea.

On one occasion, Gin resorted to pure cunning in her determination to resume normal activities. The boys were away camping for the weekend and I had taken the girls shopping while the baby slept. Dan had office work to finish, so Gin settled down in the living room all by herself to listen to records.

Every little while, Dan would check on her; she was happily coloring while she listened to the music. The co-ordination it took to change the records was good therapy for her fingers, and it pleased her that she could handle them without needing someone's help.

Dan, busy at his desk, could hear the music of "Peter and the Wolf," "Hansel and Gretel," "Sound of Music," and "Mary Poppins," and "Mary Poppins," and "Mary Poppins," and "Mary Poppins."

All of a sudden it registered with him; that same song had been playing over and over again. He went to the living room to check. Ginny was gone.

"Gin, where are you? Gin! Ginny!" A quick tour through the house got no answer from her.

He ran outside and shouted, "Gin! Ginny!"

Two hundred feet down the sidewalk, he saw her . . . crawling to visit "Aunt Alice."

He helped her back to the house, and gave her a stern lecture on why she—or any of the kids—was not allowed to take off without permission. Sheepishly, she crawled back to the record player, and changed "Mary Poppins."

Dan tried to reconstruct how she had managed to do it. She must have crawled through the kitchen, unhooked the back door—using a broom handle—slid down the back steps, and crawled down the sidewalk to Alice's. He even suspected she deliberately left the records playing so he would think she was still in the living room.

With the warm weather, she was wearing shorts, and the only damage was scraped knees from crawling on the concrete.

There was substantially more damage to Dan's nerves.

Alice still continued to help out whenever she could, often making a trip to therapy on a day when I didn't have a car. We were discussing Ginny's progress one day and Alice wondered if the local school system would send a tutor for her. I had serious doubts. First of all, none of the children had been in the public schools beyond kindergarten. Since she was not going to the public school before the accident, what right did I have to ask for a tutor now?

Alice assured me that the school system was equipped to handle homebound students like Ginny; the fact that Ginny had gone to parochial school had no bearing on their tutoring program. Now convinced of her eligibility, I had some serious doubts about her ability. Having a mother's conceit, I felt she could easily learn. But, she wasn't speaking freely and I really did not think the school would send a tutor till her training would be a little more normal. It is difficult for a mother to be objective about her own children, particularly one recovering from such a serious injury. It was apparent to me that she was extremely bright, reasonable and understanding, but would the school, or a tutor, agree?

With no confidence that she would have a teacher immediately, but with the possibility of having her name put on file for tutoring sometime in the future, I called the school.

When I started to explain the situation to the secretary who answered, she stopped me. She already knew about Ginny and was surprised I hadn't called sooner.

"But she's not able to speak—just a few words."

"It doesn't matter. She's entitled to a tutor. I'll see what I can do."

She connected me with Mr. Hrubes, the director of "Special Services." I gave him a brief history of her injury. As honestly as I could, I explained her capabilities and her limitations. He considered her situation and said he'd send a tutor in a day or two! He then said something which lifted my spirits. "When it is time for her to go back full time, don't put her in the 'special classes.' She is ill, not handicapped!"

It made me feel good that someone so knowledgeable had the same confidence as I in her capabilities and potential. To me, "ill" implied the possibility of future recovery; "handicapped" did not offer that hope. I still had that hope and was not ready even to consider, much less face the possibility, that she might not recover.

The following morning, Mrs. Garvey called. She would tutor Ginny five days a week and wanted to arrange a time schedule. She knew about Gin's accident and was anxious to work with her. Her enthusiasm reinforced my belief in Ginny's potential.

Mrs. Garvey's responsibilities to her own family kept her busy mornings; Ginny's obligations were therapy and a daily nap. It worked out best for all if Mrs. Garvey saw Ginny for an hour each day right after lunch.

I don't know what prompted me to say it, but I asked if she knew Ginny couldn't talk.

No—that hadn't been mentioned. But she would try to see if she could help her anyway. Her earlier confidence seemed suddenly to turn to apprehension.

When she arrived the next day, she looked even more apprehensive than I had imagined. A pert blonde, in her mid-twenties, with a natural warmth, she impressed me as being an ideal teacher for Gin if Gin could be taught. I was trying to bolster her courage by singing Ginny's virtues. She worked hard, listened intently and remembered everything that was said. I was sure she could be taught to read and that she would be able to read to herself. Someday when her speech came back she would be able to go back and read aloud.

Mrs. Garvey seemed rather skeptical about these attributes and my hopes, but agreed to try. Possibly she could relearn to print and by using small blocks grasp number concepts.

(I didn't see number concepts as any problem. When you have frequently set the table for nine people, numbers from one to nine are quite vivid. Before the accident Ginny and Theresa would frequently do the job together and the conversation was often, "You brought only six plates; go get three more. We have only four forks; get four more. No, that makes eight; we need five more." Just everyday living with that many people lays quite a foundation in arithmetic, especially in division when you have three candy bars to split seven ways!)

Actually, I wasn't sure how thoroughly she remembered numbers, and her writing certainly needed improvement. Her ability had progressed to being able to copy letters quite well on the blackboard, having better control of the larger muscles in her arm. The fine muscles in her fingers, however, were still not too well co-ordinated, and she had difficulty keeping letters on the lines on paper. And, she still had trouble with her vision. The left eye hadn't recovered completely and would frequently drift, giving her double vision. It must have been difficult for her to make a simple "one" on a line, if she was seeing two lines and two points to the pencil. How could she know which pencil point was supposed to touch which line? It was most fatiguing for her, but she worked diligently anyway.

Even if I was overestimating her ability to learn to read, she could certainly profit from anything that Mrs. Garvey was able to get across to her.

At the end of the first session, Mrs. Garvey was noncommittal. By the end of the second session, she had caught the same enthusiasm that we all had. Ginny could learn anything!

Mrs. Garvey's warmth was infectious. Ginny worked for her the same way she would work for anyone she loved. It was only an hour a day, but it was a tremendous effort for Gin. Mrs. Garvey constantly encouraged her and praised her, which gave Ginny the impetus to work all the harder. She wanted to be a good girl; she wanted to please. If Mrs. Garvey was pleased with her, that was all the reward she sought.

The writing improved. Her hand was getting steadier. She had a reason to keep trying, because Mrs. Garvey kept telling her she was doing better than the day before. And because she was encouraged, she did better the day after.

Mrs. Garvey was amazed at her perseverance and her desire for perfection. Things just had to be done right! The letters had to be straight and aligned or she would erase and do them over until they were all satisfactory. And typical of a child's first erasures, sometimes there were holes in the page from sweat and scrubbing.

Mrs. Garvey wondered if Ginny had always been such a perfectionist. She had. It was just part of her nature. She personified the proverb that anything worth doing is worth doing well.

In the early days of her recovery it had been predicted that she might go through a personality change. If she had a sunny disposition before, she could easily come out of the coma a belligerent, resentful child. It had seemed necessary to warn us in advance. In fact, it never happened. Her personality changed only to the extent that it was enhanced and intensified.

The satisfaction that Mrs. Garvey realized was just as deep as ours. Any new ability she achieved was a victory; any knowledge gained, a triumph.

At the end of "class" for the day, Mrs. Garvey always brought Ginny to me and proudly encouraged her to show off any new accomplishment. "Tell Mommy the new word you can say. Show her the star you got because your writing was so neat." While Gin was basking in the glow of a new stride, Mrs. Garvey renewed my pride. "You know, Mrs. Carson, of all the pupils I've taught, Ginny offers the greatest challenge . . . and the deepest rewards. To be able to work with her is a privilege."

Although it couldn't be accomplished by ordinary methods, Mrs. Garvey was teaching her to read! She had devised a system of testing her with flash cards. It was evident that Ginny really knew the words. Possibly, I hadn't overestimated her ability.

The whole concept of "going to school" and doing homework just like the other children pleased Gin. Another step closer to normal life.

For all my courage, philosophy, faith or hope, whatever you want to call it, there were times when it was difficult. Generally it was when I was overtired almost to the point of exhaustion. It seemed that faith and fatigue did not go hand-in-hand. It was hard to rationalize why God asked so much at one time. I did, however, try to rationalize. I always compared my relationship with my children to God's relationship with me, recognizing that my concept was finite, while His was infinite.

If I had two children and one was strong, the other weak, I would expect more of the strong one. I should feel flattered that God expected so much of me. He must have felt that I had the capability of doing a little more than what might normally be asked. He must have felt that I was able to do what was necessary. It has been said that He will never ask more than we can do. But, sometimes He comes terribly close to the dividing line.

And besides, when faced with such problems, I didn't have much choice. I had a tremendous responsibility. Crying and running away weren't going to help Ginny or the other children, or Dan or myself.

The week after the accident, the gospel at Mass was of "the little girl who was not dead, only sleeping." I felt a part of the reliving of that miracle of a little girl waking up from so deep a sleep.

The Sisters at school always inquired about Ginny's progress. Whenever there was anything new to report, the other children always spread the good word. Sister Agnes had frequently invited me to bring Ginny back to the class whenever it was convenient. On the way home from therapy one day, Ginny and I stopped at St. Christopher's for a visit.

We went to the principal's office. Sister St. James was amazed. She had had the children's progress reports, but it was the first time she had seen Ginny in a long time. She still remembered that day, over seven months before, when she had seen her, almost without life, lying in the hospital.

She took us to the first-grade classroom. Sister Agnes asked Ginny if she'd like to sit down. The class had all been cued to offer Ginny no assistance in directing her to her old desk. Sister wanted to know if she remembered where she had sat in the class for those first few weeks of school.

Ginny took me right to her own desk.

The children were all happy to see her and had prepared a play. Part of the story involved picking flowers in a field. Dandelions had been scattered on the floor in the front of the room. In the midst of the other preparations, the janitor came by and nearly swept up half of their props, much to the children's consternation and Sister's and my amusement. The flower field restored, the play went on as scheduled. It was a typical first-grade play complete with forgotten lines, prompting from the "audience" and poked ribs to remind actors of cues. We all enjoyed it thoroughly. For a few minutes Ginny felt she was part of her class again.

After we left, Sister was talking to the class about their reaction to Ginny. They weren't too concerned that her hair was still "boyish," or that she could say only a few words, or needed help to walk.

Their strongest comment was, "Gee, she got big!"

***

CHAPTER 20

I HAD BECOME INCREASINGLY CONCERNED ABOUT ROBERTA. I HAD compared notes with my sister-in-law because her baby was exactly the same age, but her answers were always a little evasive. I would mention that I wasn't satisfied with her weight gain and ability, but I never told anyone the thing I suspected.

She was due to go to Dr. Metcalf for a regular check up. She was now eight and a half months old. I had no qualms about just laying her on the seat of the car. She couldn't roll over. Throughout the drive, I kept mentally rephrasing my question.

Finally, in his office, there just seemed no subtle or delicate way of asking. As simply as I could, I questioned, "Is she retarded?"

I must have broken his heart. He had been our doctor for so long, had seen us through so much with Ginny this past year. How could he tell me?

The truth was—he couldn't! There just was no way he could bring himself to place one more burden on my shoulders. He tried to lead me into it gently with, "She certainly seems so, at times." He rechecked the records of her PKU test done at birth. It was a comparatively new test that revealed some forms of retardation. Hers was "negative."

Roberta's hip joints were very loose. Her legs would flop out at 90-degree angles with her body. The joints tended to suck in. He suspected that there might also be a problem of a congenital hip deformity, and suggested that I take her to see the orthopedic specialists who had put the casts on Ginny after her accident.

Dr. Kozinn examined Roberta, made various tests to check her response and took X rays. They were developed immediately. He came back with the reports and sat down to talk to me.

He seemed upset and nervous, most unlike the self-assured personality I remembered from when he worked with Ginny. It was difficult for him to try to tell me. He said that the X ray showed all the bones to be perfectly normal. For the moment I was relieved, but still wondered about his being so deeply disturbed. Then he started talking about "Down's syndrome."

I did not know what "Down's syndrome" meant, and wasn't following what he was telling me, but recognized that he was having the same difficulty as Dr. Metcalf. He knew too much about our problems with Ginny to try to tell me what was wrong with Roberta.

Finally I said, "Doctor, I've suspected that she is a Mongoloid."

Then he opened up. He said he wasn't positive, but she had many of the characteristics. He thought it would be best if we had a chromosome test done to confirm it.

Within a week, I was in a neurologist's office, waiting while he was examining her. A studious, intent man, he said little while he conducted his examination.

Then he sat down and showed that same hesitancy I had seen twice before. There was no tactful way for him to say it. How did he know how I would react?

When he realized that, in my own heart, I already knew and accepted it, it seemed to upset him even more. He may have been afraid that I was putting up a front and was suddenly going to break. Maybe a "normal" mother's reaction is to rebel, and my resignation was unnerving. It seemed that I ended up consoling him because he had to be the one to tell me.

I had suspected it for so long. Her eyes had a little slant, but so did Paul's as an infant, and his eventually straightened.

She had constant respiratory problems, but Ginny had them too, until she was three and had her tonsils removed.

She was so limp, but I reasoned that the hole in her heart prevented her from getting an adequate supply of oxygen; she would not be as energetic or lively as another child.

Through the past months, I had mentally been over all her shortcomings, her lethargy and her heart problem. Now that I had confirmation of the truth, it was much easier. It was one explanation to all the problems I had been aware of. They were all symptoms of Mongolism—which I now knew was correctly called "Down's syndrome." I was actually relieved to have a firm diagnosis.

Alice knew where I had gone that day. As I drove up, she just "happened to be walking by." She always seemed to know when I needed her—when it was good to have someone to talk to. When I told her, she admitted that several of the neighbors who had cared for Roberta when Ginny was in the hospital were aware of the baby's retardation but not one could tell me. They all thought that I did not suspect it. For months we each had been carrying the burden; they not wanting to tell me—I not wanting to voice my fears because I could have been wrong and I had already brought so much grief to my friends.

Now it was easier for everyone.

It seemed to hit my sister-in-law the hardest. But when I finished telling her, she paid us a high compliment. "If it had to be, it's good she has you and Dan for parents."

More than that, it was good she had our whole family. They all deeply loved her. And who would understand better than Ginny how difficult it is to walk and talk!

Besides, I never had a baby I could simply enjoy and play with. The older children being a year apart, I had always had two or three babies at once. There had never been just one little baby to enjoy thoroughly. What with going to the hospital to see Ginny every day for those five months, I had missed so much time with Roberta. It was good that she would be a baby for a long time!

✳ ✳ ✳

CHAPTER 21

GINNY KEPT IMPROVING. BUT PEOPLE WOULD OFTEN QUESTION "WHY did it have to happen to an innocent little child? How could God let something so tragic come about?"

I kept relying on my system of rationalization. Sometimes I made my children do things they could not understand, because I knew it was for an ultimate good. God often asked things that we didn't understand—that were for an ultimate good. Sometimes we learned the reason; sometimes it was obscure. But, certainly God's judgment was better than mine.

There were many good things which came from the experience of Ginny's accident. Many were spiritual and idealistic; others, though material and most practical on the surface, contained the underlying element of sincere thoughtfulness.

The friends she had made in the hospital who had promised to visit, did, even though they had families and responsibilities of their own. The two little girls who shared the room with Ginny kept their word and came to see her. It had not been just a passing "hospital relationship." They had formed a deep friendship. The father of the baby who had been so ill would stop on his way home from work, or bring some of his other children to visit her. Ginny still checked to find the treat he always brought in his pocket. His wife called and, although she wasn't free to leave because their little fellow was still ill, assured me that someday during the summer we'd have to bring all the children to swim in their pool.

The gifts that came for Ginny were selected carefully. A woman in my father's office checked on her progress regularly. When she learned Ginny was regaining the co-ordination in her hands, she found a set of large beads that snapped together to make necklaces.

As Ginny's balance became better, a volunteer at the hospital overheard that Ginny did not have a bike. Three days later a beautiful bicycle was delivered.

The toys were perfect—each chosen to be on a level with her progress and thus encourage her to do more.

Many friends sent new outfits for her, knowing that she had outgrown all her clothing. Now, because of their thoughtfulness, she was acquiring the most chic wardrobe any little girl could want.

A long-time friend of Dan's parents stopped to visit but had underestimated the reports on Ginny's growth. The slacks she brought just weren't going to fit. Noticing that Bernadette was now a size smaller than Gin, the solution was clear. She decided that Dettie, too, deserved some new clothes. Dettie was delighted, and in a few days Ginny received another package, two more slack sets—a size larger.

My father had a "nodding acquaintance" with a businesswoman as they waited each morning at the Baldwin railroad station for the same train. One morning shortly after Ginny's accident, by chance, they sat together and talked during the trip to New York City. Although they had been saying "Good morning" for years, they did not know each other's names. In the conversation, she mentioned the tragic accident in which two little girls were involved and that one was still recovering. Dad told her it was his granddaughter.

When they reached the city, she insisted that he wait a minute while she went into a store and bought a "little candy" for his grandchildren. He waited while she shopped. She returned with a bagful of "goodies for the children." When I opened the package, there was also an envelope containing the means "to get something for Ginny."

Through the months, she kept inquiring of Gin's progress. At Easter, she sent more candy, and another "treat for Ginny." Her generosity seemed limitless.

The woman who had sent that basket of flowers when Ginny first came home had a sister who had promised to give a check to a needy mission, if she were able to see the solution to a particular problem. After much prayer, the problem was resolved. She felt she owed a debt. She knew about Ginny, and decided that ours was the "neediest mission" she knew. Her check had paid for the excursion to see *The Sound of Music.*

Having lived in the same town all my life, there were many who knew me since childhood. In some cases, my classmates had moved away, but their parents had stayed. With daughters my age, and grandchildren Ginny's age, the story about the accident seemed to touch more closely.

One friend had had seven children of her own. The previous summer she had invited me to bring my family for lunch and a swim at her rather elegant home. I hesitated. She encouraged, "What can your children do that mine didn't?"

Throughout Ginny's illness she checked on her progress. Knowing when she was regaining the use of her hands, she brought scissors, construction paper and crayons. Remembering what treasures these were to her own children, there was an ample supply for all my little ones. "School" was in session, with Bernadette "teaching" and Ginny and Celia as "pupils." The bright colors of the paper, and "teacher's" assigned "art projects" gave Ginny the incentive to relearn to control scissors.

Another friend had a way of uniting the spiritual with the material. She would send Mass cards with a check enclosed "to get something special for the children." Often it was the means of accomplishing something that otherwise would have been left undone.

Frequently cards would come with a check enclosed with a note "For a treat." Whenever I could, these were used for little extras, but often the "treat" turned out to be two cases of milk or a pair of needed shoes. These gifts helped so much.

I hope and pray that God will reward all of them for their generosity at a time when it was so desperately needed!

❋❋❋

CHAPTER 22

By early June, more than eight months after the accident, Ginny's speech was finally coming back! There were more and more words she could say and now had mastered several "useful sentences." "I am hungry." "I am thirsty." Her favorite sentence was "I can tie my shoe" although she really couldn't tie shoelaces yet.

She was able to dress herself completely, except for tying the shoes, and was frequently able to do larger buttons.

Her walking was improving. Previously, she walked by holding furniture and supporting herself against the walls. Now she was able to do short stretches on her own. The falls were less frequent. She was learning to regain her balance, or catch herself safely on the nearest piece of furniture. It was quite shaky—but it was progress.

Her brother John took it upon himself to help her practice. He would back away a few paces, and she would walk to him. As he backed up a little further, she would extend the distance. After many practice sessions, he called me. "Want to see what Ginny can do?" He had cleared an open path from the front door, through the hall, all the way across the living room, a distance of about forty feet. She started at the front door. He stayed abreast of her, catching her if she seemed about to fall. When she reached the end of the run, I praised both of them. John shrugged it off with, "She did it better last time. I had to catch her only once."

It was scary to watch. Her gait was comparable to that of a drunk trying to walk on a ship's pitching deck. She would get giddy with excitement and accomplishment, and break up laughing so hard that she had no balance at all. Her laugh was infectious and John would also begin to laugh, but he would sober up sooner than she and almost scold her, "Come on, Ginny. You've got to be serious. You've got to learn to walk, so that when you go to therapy you can show them you are getting better."

He kept working with her, until he had her walking the full length "all by herself, without catching her at all!"

Gin had always loved to swim and it was finally warm enough to set up the backyard pool. It was only 2½ feet deep and 12 feet across, so she felt safe in it. Before the accident, she swam like a fish. In therapy, her "swimming" in the Hubbard Tank required someone to support her under her armpits to keep her head up.

She wanted to try swimming on her own. I wondered what would happen.

Paul and John had finished swimming and were standing just outside of the pool. As I watched from the kitchen window, I really didn't know what to expect. She had been such a good swimmer but she still was lacking so much co-ordination.

As Dan lifted her in I found myself asking again, "Dear God, please. . . ." She stood by the side, holding it for support. The water came almost to her waist. She took a breath and dived, as if nothing had ever happened.

In a moment she was swallowing water and couldn't get to her feet. The two boys were with her in a split second.

They did beautifully! They helped her to her feet, let her cough out the water and before she had a chance to be afraid they started giving her a "ride" around the pool. "Come on, Gin, you can do it." In a few minutes, she was splashing happily with just a little support from her brothers. And as always in joy, I filled with tears.

School was dismissed for the summer for the older children, although her tutor, Mrs. Garvey, arranged to see Ginny twice a week for several weeks to make up for some missed days. She felt that it was better to continue the tutoring over a few more weeks, to shorten the period until it would begin again in the fall. She was afraid if Ginny's vacation was too long, she might forget all they had gained.

Ginny's work had progressed, although she had come nowhere near making up that whole first year in the six weeks of tutoring. She was doing well with her arithmetic and the writing continued to become more and more steady. The reading seemed to be improving, but was still hampered by her limited speech.

Mrs. Garvey's energy knew no bounds. She always stressed Ginny's accomplishments—better writing, a new word that she could say, a whole sentence that she could read, an arithmetic paper that had gotten a "100." Her constant encouragement inspired Ginny and reinforced me. Gin could learn; it would just take time— more time than I had anticipated.

She had been such an ideal teacher for Ginny that it was another disappointment when she told me she wouldn't be coming back in September. She was going to teach full time and Ginny would get a new tutor. Reminding myself of the transition from Raleigh to Rita, I hoped it would go as smoothly.

With all the children home for the summer, life was delightful. Their companionship and stimulation were good for Ginny. As always, when school closes for vacation, I was relieved. I can't stand schedules. They never allow for all the little things that come up. Freedom from routine was wonderful. And besides, the children really are helpful around the house. They all have their jobs to do and we work together on major projects. The summer before, we had built a retaining wall from the back walk to the driveway. There was another stretch about a hundred feet long that could use a similar wall. Because things were different this year, I was reluctant to tackle it. The boys talked me into giving it a try.

The year before we had moved our garage. The old driveway was the source of concrete. Smashed into convenient sizes, it became the "rocks" we needed to complete the wall. The boys broke the concrete with sledge hammers, pried it loose with crowbars and hauled it in wheelbarrows. The girls helped with the lighter digging, leveling and packing of earth between the layers. Ginny worked right along with the rest of the children, though the boys often considered her "job" as riding back in the empty wheelbarrow for another load of rocks. Around the neighborhood, the project became known as the "Great Wall of Carson" and other children frequently came to offer their services. In spite of the hard work and sweat involved, they really enjoyed doing something so massive. When the project was completed, the children were all justifiably proud of a fine stone wall, which they themselves had built.

The regular household chores weren't nearly as much fun as building the wall and often the boys would con the girls into doing the dishes for them so they could work outside. But they each had responsibilities, often helping each other to make jobs go quicker. Ginny usually managed to be the "ringleader." She would work right along with the others—alternately encouraging and prodding anyone not doing his share.

Generally when it was her turn to do the dishes, I'd work with her. One evening, however, I had to finish transplanting some young seedlings that I had ambitiously dug out in the afternoon. Since I'd be working right outside the kitchen door, I left her to start the dishes on her own. She was agreeable and went happily about clearing the table.

I was almost finished outside when I heard a chilling scream that sent me flying to her side. She stood holding two glasses in each hand. They were starting to slip from her grasp and with her attention drawn to the glasses she could not co-ordinate her legs to walk. It was hard to tell if she was more afraid of falling or of dropping and smashing the glasses. But there was no question that she had to concentrate to make movements we all perform automatically.

She settled down and I started washing the dishes. When I turned around, she was off on a new tack. She previously had been sweeping the floor by using a brush broom and the dustpan, crawling around to do the job. Now she decided that she was going to sweep the floor, standing up!

After the incident of almost dropping the glasses, it seemed that she could use a new confidence-builder, and this might be the answer. She set off to tackle her project. She would get her balance and sweep what she could reach. Then she would move her footing to a better location and sweep again. She completed the whole job with the regular broom. She was thrilled, and so was I. I was holding her, telling her what a good girl she was. She looked up at me and said, "And when I'm bad, I'm *very* bad."

She had made the most concise evaluation of her own personality. All she needed was the "curl in the middle of her forehead." Most of the time she was happy and industrious. But when she was tired, she could go completely to pieces and be absolutely inconsolable. There was no alternative but to make her take a nap. When she woke, she'd often tell me, "The 'bad Ginny' went away and the 'good Ginny' is back."

The volunteer who had given her the bicycle knew it was often difficult for me to get Ginny to the hospital for therapy. She took it upon herself to pick Ginny up and bring her home on Tuesdays. Although it made her trip to work several miles longer, she insisted, "It's right on my way."

Gin had done the sweeping job on Monday evening. On the way to therapy the next morning, she told the volunteer all about it. At the hospital, the volunteer related the story to Rita. By the end of the therapy session, the merits of the "good Ginny" deserved special praise. Rita skipped lunch and rode along with the volunteer to bring Gin home. Both came in and Gin glowed with pride in her accomplishment as she demonstrated how she swept the floor.

Rita's giving up her lunch hour was another example of her delight in sharing the enthusiasm of Ginny's progesss. And Ginny was progressing. Rita was able to reduce the therapy sessions to twice a week!

Her speech was a delight. It had been so long in coming that we appreciated it that much more. She could now actually converse. She often had difficulty remembering the exact word she wanted, but she was able to explain what she intended to say. If she couldn't say a word composed of sounds she couldn't make, like "garage," she would substitute "the place where Daddy puts the car," which was made up of simpler sounds.

Frank Volz, her speech therapist, had been seeing her three times a week, for over seven months. He was warm, patient and encouraging, even though her speech showed the slowest recovery. While she worked willingly for the others, because of seemingly insurmountable difficulties in relearning the speech she so desperately wanted, she often rebelled against Frank. He had always been good to her and I could never understand why she frequently did not want to work for him. He made games out of the speech lessons and often she "won" dimes for her efforts. He was constantly praising and encouraging her, yet still she balked.

Now that she was at the hospital only twice a week, Frank came to the house every Friday to keep the third appointment. He'd devise ways that Celia and Bernadette could work with Gin; he'd even rig the rules of the games so Gin could "beat them at words." Still she stubbornly refused to even be nice to him.

She was a "Mary Poppins" fan and we used to tell her that when she could say "supercalifragilistic . . ." she wouldn't need speech therapy any more. At the time, it seemed so far off, so high a goal, that it was a safe promise. I was sure that by the time she was able to say all that, she would have mastered everything else. She played the "Mary Poppins" record frequently and I didn't suspect anything beyond the fact that she enjoyed the music. But, she was practicing.

Frank arrived at the door for a regular therapy session. Before he was two steps inside, she was standing there.

She took a deep breath . . . "Sup-er-cal-i-fra-gil-is-tic-ex-pi-al-i-do-cious! Now you go!"

But, speech therapy continued three times a week. There was still a lot of work to be done, but as it became easier, and as the speech became more fluent, she enjoyed it much more.

Because of her intensive training, in some ways her diction became clearer than the other children's. I often wondered if Frank had the wrong pupil. For example, Celia insisted that the boys played "fitball." From the intensity with which they played, possibly she was more accurate.

***

CHAPTER 23

CHARITY IS NOT CONFINED TO ANY RELIGION; IT IS UNIVERSAL. IN ALL the world, it is the greatest hope for unity and peace among peoples. Ginny's injury touched the hearts of many and led them all toward working and praying for one common cause. Maybe, in some small way, this whole experience was a step toward unity.

Many months after the accident, I was introduced to a woman who questioned my name. Was I the Carson whose little girl had been hit by a truck? She lived only a few houses from the accident scene. That afternoon she was waiting for her daughters to come home from school. She heard someone scream that two little girls had been hit by a truck and ran frantically to the corner.

It was a relief to find that her children were all right.

She described her one little girl as being very unemotional, almost hard. Nothing seemed to impress or move her. She had come home from school several days later, having walked with Celia.

She came in, told her mother how severely Ginny was hurt, how much Ginny's little sister cared . . . then broke down and cried.

Her mother said it was the only time she ever remembered her being moved to tears.

Compassion is a beautiful thing.

The progress continued, slowly, but constantly. No one appreciated it more than Ginny herself.

She stood holding a small rubber ball, bounced it and tried to catch it. Who could count how many times she missed, how many times she crawled after it? One day she cheered for herself. "I can do it! I can do it!"

She became more and more aware of her limitations and while this led to some frustration for her, it also made her increase her efforts to overcome them. Although it seems like such a small thing, one accomplishment that still eluded her was tying her shoes. She simply could not make her fingers work the laces into a bow.

One afternoon I was sorting some wash on the kitchen table. Roberta was sleeping and the other children were in school. Ginny was upstairs in her room and I was just half listening for her in case she needed me.

Suddenly, Ginny let out a shriek that almost stopped my heart. I raced up the stairs two at a time and found her sitting on the edge of her bed, eyes wide, face flushed, and trembling all over with excitement.

"I-can-do-it," she announced, enunciating every syllable clearly. "I-could-do-it-before-I-was-hit-and-I-can-do-it-NOW!"

"Do what, Gin?" I asked in relief.

She pointed to her shoe, tied with a floppy bow.

With great pride and a new emphasis she said, "Now-I-*can*-tie-my-shoe!"

I often wondered how much she actually remembered of the hospital experience, particularly of the early months.

Roberta was slow eating. Ginny was watching me feeding her one day and instructed, "You should sing to her. Know why? When I was hit with the truck, you fed me baby food and you used to sing to me."

She had been eating baby food in January. Did she remember anything before that? Whenever she described her hospital room, it always had several windows. The private room had only one. The move to the big room was in January.

One day I thought I had a dramatic breakthrough. We were talking about her hospital stay. Thinking about how warm the pediatric ward was kept, I asked her if she were hot or cold when she was sick. "I was very cold. Know why? I had no clothes on!"

I was positive she was remembering those first weeks! I had never spoken to her or the other children about the fact that she wasn't dressed at first. (Much of her information she got from the other children, but I knew I had never mentioned that particular fact to any of them, being afraid it might upset them.) Her knowing about it proved to me that she had some memory of the first five weeks.

Some days later, I was looking at pictures that a medical magazine had made for a story on the use of hypothermia (the ice-blanket treatment) showing Ginny during her first weeks in the hospital. She was wearing no clothes in the pictures.

My proof was shattered. She had looked at the pictures.

It seemed that she had no memory of the first two months, and only knew scattered parts of the rest of the stay in the hospital. Most of it I was sure she "remembered" because she had overheard our conversations, or simply because when she asked, we told her.

Our living room was very large and of a shape that could only have been built in an eighty-year-old house. It was basically long and narrow. One wall had a massive built-in cabinet making that end even narrower, and another wall opened into an old-fashioned sun parlor. I had tried many times to figure out how the floor could be covered with rugs. Although I love to do intricate jigsaw puzzles, there was no combination of commercial sized rugs that would fit. They either overlapped each other and flapped up the walls, or they left so much open floor space that they would look like scattered scatter rugs.

The floor had been covered with wall-to-wall carpet which had constant traffic for fifteen years. It was now worn through the backing and padding right to the bare wood. I had been removing throw rugs from bedrooms and covering the holes. This gave it the appearance of a patchwork quilt. The little mats were forever slipping out of place, leaving holes as well as little rugs to trip over.

There was no inexpensive solution. We had to get new carpeting. There was just too much risk that Ginny would fall. She was having enough difficulty staying on her feet without creating an obstacle course for her to cross.

I went shopping. The salesman inquired how the room was used. I explained that we had eight children who all played in the living room. The TV was there, so the floor was often covered with sprawled bodies. It was the thoroughfare from the kitchen to the front stairs.

He stopped showing me delicate wool broadlooms and suggested that I consider commercial carpet—the kind used in stores, theater lobbies and any place that gets unreasonable abuse.

There was one that would have been ideal. We figured yardage, padding, installation. I thanked him and suggested that I go talk it over with Dan.

Driving home, I wondered if I could tack down the throw rugs. We just did not have the five hundred dollars. Dan had been saving the change out of his pockets for months and it was quite a bottle full. I had a check for seventy-five dollars, pay for secretarial work I had done for my bowling league. Together it might have made two hundred dollars. We would just have to keep saving for a while and hope that no one broke a leg in the meantime.

During this summer the children had become conscious of the inadequacy of our pool. It was twelve feet across and Paul was now almost six feet tall. They frequently asked if we could get a big one. I would tell them to just be grateful that they had a place to cool off in—and further limit the number of children swimming at one time. If they went one or two at a time, it wasn't too crowded.

They decided to collect all their funds and start saving. But their ambition soared; instead of a plastic one, they wanted to get a built-in pool. They rooted through their rooms, searched out all their hiding places. The kitchen table was cleared and soon looked like an old-fashioned public countinghouse. There were bankbooks, some having as much as twenty-seven dollars, saved from First Communion and birthday gifts. There was pay from mowing lawns and doing odd jobs around the neighborhood.

Most of it was in change. They found empty boxes and sorted all the coins. The counting went on and on, each total differing from the one previously reached. Finally they arrived at the same sum twice and established a total, almost two hundred dollars between them. They decided that if all kept adding anything they had available, worked more conscientiously on odd jobs and saved faithfully, they would, in a few years' time, be able to save two thousand dollars.

The goal seemed far off to me, and I wondered if the enthusiasm would dwindle. I was, however, glad to see them all working together for a common cause.

Several weeks later, one of the children discovered Dan's "bank" full of change and wondered if it could be added to the pool fund. After all, "You and Mom like to swim, too."

Dan explained he was saving for a new carpet for the living room. Nothing more was said.

Soon afterward, I was walking through the room, carrying Roberta. Most of the children were around. I caught my heel in one of the holes in the rug. I didn't fall but it could have been disastrous. Evidently, it had been critically observed.

Still, nothing was said, but the children must have had a "meeting." After supper they all came with their box of money so religiously saved for a pool.

"Mommy almost fell today. You need a new rug more than we need a pool. If you put Daddy's rug fund with it, will you have enough?"

There was another "counting session." There was almost four hundred dollars. The next day was Labor Day. We started looking through the Sunday papers. A carpet store nearby was having a "Holiday Special." First thing, the next morning, I went to see if there was anything suitable.

The room needed a blue carpet to tie it all together. There was one blue sample, on sale, and within our fund.

I ordered it and the children were just as anxious for delivery as I was. When it was installed, it was beautiful. They decided *they* owned the carpet; Dan and I owned the pad and installation.

As long as it was their carpet, I suggested they keep it clean. It was agreed; it was "our" carpet.

✸✸✸

CHAPTER 24

As it always does for me, summer went quickly, much too quickly, and it was time for school again. I hoped that this year would go well.

There is probably something wrong with me that I'm not delighted to have all the children out of the house for a few hours. But, I find that the panic of getting them out and the headaches over homework are so great that it's not worth it. Probably if I were more systematic, better organized, and regimented, it would work. But, I'm convinced that there is a basic mathematical formula that states that the confusion in a household is directly proportional to the square of the number of children.

As hard as I wished that summer vacation would last forever, school began.

Ginny had to make a regular visit to Dr. Rosenzweig. He reviewed one major problem that still existed. While in the hospital, they had made a test to determine if there had been any permanent damage to her kidneys from the hemorrhaging at the time of the accident. The test showed a partial obstruction in a tube between one kidney and her bladder, causing the kidney to drain inadequately. It was decided that it would require surgery, but not at that time. There was too much risk that an operation would set back her recovery from the accident. She was put on a medication and the operation had been postponed.

Now Dr. Rosenzweig felt she was recovering well enough that

the urologist should see her again. He was not saying that she was ready for surgery; he just wanted the kidney condition checked.

When she walked into the urologist's office, he was pleased. He had not seen Ginny since the early days when she was still unconscious! After examining her, he decided that the condition was not getting any worse, and again postponed the operation, possibly until the following spring.

It seems that in every family there is one child whom you have more difficulty reaching. Ours was John. He could be impossible. Yet, he overheard a conversation regarding Ginny's impending operation. He came to me afterward, "Will they have to take out Ginny's kidney?"

"I don't know, John. It depends on what they find when they operate."

He considered that for a moment, then explained why he had asked. "I saw a show one time where one brother donated a kidney to another. If Ginny needs one, would you let me give her one of mine?"

Moments like that overwhelmed me—and gave me new hope!

It was again time to see the public school regarding Ginny's education. She was doing well, but it would have been most difficult for her to attend regular classes. Her walking was getting better, although she still had the "foot drop" in her right foot that made it necessary for her to step high when she walked. She just could not lift those toes. In making plans for the school year, I had tried again to get a prediction from Dr. Holtzman, wondering if she would be walking well enough later in the year. He wouldn't promise if it would ever return, but added, "I don't know why I hesitate now. She's done everything else I said she couldn't do!"

So, her walking was still too slow to cope with eight hundred other children, and I had no real expectancy of so drastic an improvement in the forseeable future. Because she would be going into the hospital sometime during the school year, it was decided it would be best to plan on a tutor for that whole year, and not consider her going back to school until she could stay.

The new tutor, Miss Engel, arrived in mid-September. She was tall and thin, had dark hair and glasses, giving her a scholarly appearance. I guessed that it hadn't been very long since she was the student instead of the teacher.

She worked with Ginny later in the afternoon, and it had the advantage that Gin could take a nap before "school" time and begin her class thoroughly refreshed.

Like Mrs. Garvey, Miss Engel had great patience and understanding. And she obviously was very familiar with the role of student, devising ways to keep the studies fun. One day she brought apples, settled Ginny and herself in the middle of the floor, and they had a "picnic" while they did their reading. Ginny always looked forward to her coming and was most anxious to work with her.

Her speech had improved to a point where we were correcting grammar. Earlier she would say, "I not know." Now she was starting to interrupt herself, and rephrase it to "I do not know" or "I do not remember."

Miss Engel started using the reader Gin had from the previous semester but ran into a problem. Ginny had it memorized. She was reciting it, without the book, and had it down so smoothly that she even knew when to turn the pages.

Before the accident, Ginny had an unusual ability for memorization. She had been able to recite many poems word for word, and knew all her favorite records perfectly. Her recitation of the reader was a good indication that the power hadn't been impaired, but it was no help in her relearning to read.

Miss Engel got a different set of readers and began anew.

In many ways, Ginny had a normal seven-year-old response to schoolwork. Some things she grasped readily; others were difficult. The math came easily but the reading appeared insurmountable at times. It seemed that part of the problem was related to the difficulty she had relearning to speak. She still had trouble with the double vision making the shape of a word apparently change as she studied it. Often she became discouraged, but continued to try.

In mid-October, some of Alice's children were going to a "play" at their school. Alice invited Ginny to come. At first she had been enthusiastic, but, as the day wore on, she decided that she did not want to go. Finally, she confided, "I don't want to go because I won't be able to *play* with them."

I explained that a "play" was a show something like a movie, but with real people. She could sit with the other children and watch. The enthusiasm all flooded back.

It was the first time I realized how much she recognized her own limitations and what effort she would exert to avoid situations where she was afraid that she would not "fit in."

It was again October 25, a full year since the day of the accident. We were talking about it. Ginny was in on the conversation and quipped, "Should I sing 'Happy Birthday' to the truck?"

By the beginning of November, her right foot was markedly improved. She could lift the toes quite far, almost up to a position at right angles with her leg. Because it took a deliberate concentrated effort to move the foot, it did not yet facilitate her walking, but it was an obvious improvement in an area that had seemed at a standstill.

By mid-November, her therapy sessions were reduced to one a week!

Thanksgiving was upon us. The children all helped and we moved the table into the living room, got out the good china and candles. As at every holiday, my father's friend from the train had sent a shopping bagful of a "little candy for the children," and this time included a bottle of wine for us. We had prepared a big turkey with all the trimmings. Mom and Dad had dinner with us. The children's table manners, if not flawless, were at least moderately good.

Having all eight children gathered around the table, having achieved so much since the Thanksgiving before, we had many blessings for which we all were deeply grateful.

Christmas was coming all too quickly. I tried to encourage the children to "do" rather than to just "buy." They all helped and we baked and froze box after box of cookies. By Christmas, we had enough for gifts all around the family. They helped make decorations for the tree and cut out snowflakes for the windows.

Holidays are happiest when a family is together. Having known the hurt of separation the year before, this Christmas was special.

Each year the children of the neighborhood went caroling, house to house, around the block. And each year the next younger of our children was eligible to go along. That year was Ginny's turn. It was a long, cold walk and her legs tired quickly. Paul and Alice's husband, Lee, who was Gin's godfather, took turns carrying her on their shoulders. What her legs lacked in endurance, her singing voice outdid in volume. The whole neighborhood was wished a most exuberant "Merry Christmas!"

Many friends sent gifts to Ginny, but the most poignant came from that same friend who rode the train with my Dad. She sent a walking doll wearing a ribbon which read, "Cross at the green—not in between!"

As they prepared for Christmas, there were many whispered discussions between the children. Little ones would come home from school with a look of pride and escaping secrecy, disappear upstairs, and come back voicing instructions, "Don't look in our bottom drawer under the pajamas!"

One afternoon, the two older boys gathered all the children upstairs. I could hear a buzz of hushed conversation. The little girls came down with a look of having been sworn to confidence. The boys took off to the village.

There was still no explanation for the boys' shopping trip. Then they left the room and returned with a huge box that had all the earmarks of being painstakingly wrapped by several boys. Inside was another box, and another, and on and on till the last box contained two smaller boxes—one labeled "Dad" and the other "Mom." Inside were two trophies for the "world's greatest father" and the "world's greatest mother."

And they came from the "world's greatest kids."

✳✳✳

CHAPTER 25

FROM ALL THE PAST EXPERIENCE, I SHOULD HAVE LEARNED TO BE ON guard when things seemed to settle down. It was simply another calm before another storm. However, after the previous hurricanes, this one seemed only a small squall.

Late one night, Dan had just finished taking a shower. He noticed something bright red spilled on the floor. His first reaction was that one of the children must have knocked over some red ink, and most assuredly would have a good explanation for needing red ink in the bathroom. The most likely suspect was Gin. Her co-ordination was improving, but frequently, when trying something difficult, her hand would start to tremble, and whatever she was holding would slip from her grasp. He made a mental note to ask her about the ink next morning.

Suddenly he realized that the pool was getting larger, and started checking for its source. He had burst a small vein in his leg and it was his blood spraying out onto the floor.

It was well after midnight and it didn't seem a big enough emer-gency to call the doctor. (Never having called a doctor between 10 P.M. and 7 A.M., although sometimes tempted to, I wondered just what it would take for me to feel justified in disturbing his sleep. But, I'd rather not find out.)

We elevated the leg and applied compresses until the bleeding stopped. After the leg was wrapped in elastic bandages, he had a cup of tea and slept through the night.

The next morning I called the surgeon. Because of a varicosity several years ago, the doctor had removed a vein in Dan's other leg. He had been watching this one, waiting for a time convenient for Dan. It, too, had to be removed. But the vein hadn't checked with Dan's schedule.

As soon as there was a bed available, he was in the hospital, right around the corner from pediatrics. Word soon spread that "Ginny's daddy" had been admitted and there was a constant parade to visit him. The first question was always, "How's Ginny?" He soon had the feeling that he could have bled to death and no one would have noticed, just as long as Ginny was okay.

Dr. French had been Ginny's anesthesiologist the day of the accident. He heard that Dan was scheduled, and asked to be put on his operation. He came to see Dan the evening before. At the time of the accident, medically Ginny could not have lived through the night. When she was still alive the next morning, Dr. French had come back to see her. He kept coming back, several times a day . . . every day. At that time I didn't fully understand his lasting interest. His work was finished.

His conversation with Dan explained all those visits. He said, "Ever since I worked on Ginny, whenever someone says something is 'hopeless,' I tell them I knew a little girl one time . . ."

It was the sixth time this surgeon had operated on someone in our family. We saw him more often than some of our relatives. He called when the operation was over. The vein was removed and everything was fine, but painful. Even after all we had been through with Ginny, no matter how medically "simple" an operation was considered, I still worried and was greatly relieved when the doctor called. It seemed it was not so important what the operation was, as who it was.

I went right over to see Dan. He was in the usual condition after surgery—in pain, tired, able to move only with difficulty. My being there seemed to be tiring him even more. I suggested that I leave so he could rest. He took my hand and asked me to stay for a while.

Because of the importance of forcing blood into veins which must take over the work of those removed, it was necessary for Dan to get up often. The first session was painful, even though he knew what to expect. Each time he got out of bed, it was a little easier. However, standing up brought on violent headaches. His bed had been designed by someone who never believed that men grow taller than 5 feet 6 inches. Dan was 6 feet 3. Every time he moved he either hit his aching head or his sore leg. Forty-eight hours after they operated, he was discharged.

As the days progressed, the leg seemed to be healing but the head-aches were getting worse. The doctor recommended a medication and quipped, "As long as his head hurts more, you know the leg is all right."

When he was more comfortable, Ginny decided he should have company. "Daddy used to come see me all the time when I was sick. Can I go read to him—like he read to me?"

She settled herself next to him in bed, propped against his shoul-der, sharing his ginger ale. Dan teased her, "What are you doing with my soda?"

"It's okay. When I was in the hospital, you used to drink *my* soda!"

Glad to have one more proof of her memory, he suffered through the paining leg, the aching head, the splashed ginger ale, and often-repeated renditions of "See Ann run. Run, run, Ann. Oh, Ann. You can run."

And Dan wondered if we would every see Ginny run.

❊❊❊

CHAPTER 26

EARLY IN FEBRUARY, GINNY WAS PRACTICING COMING DOWN THE stairs without holding the rail. She started by trying just the last step. Next the two bottom steps. Then turned around to go back up to try three. She stood there, looking down, and started to tremble. Full of her usual optimism, she admitted, "It's a little scary—but I'm going to *try*." She stood a few seconds more, then asked aloud, "God, please help me."

She made it, but decided that was enough for one day.

She still was receiving speech therapy at home, and was finally co-operating, if not enthusiastically, at least agreeably. Dan over-heard her working with flash cards, identifying pictures with an increasingly difficult vocabulary. Frank Volz praised her because she was getting them all right. He told her what a good girl she was. She said, "Yes. Now give me a *hard* one."

Ginny's schoolwork was progressing slowly—very slowly. Miss Engel had worked hard, but no matter how she tried, Ginny just did not seem able to grasp the reading. The math came easily, the writing and spelling were improving, but the reading just seemed a lost cause.

Then once more, we had to change tutors. Miss Engel had to take over a program to which she had been originally assigned at school, now getting under way.

Mr. Hrubes, the Director of Special Education Services, called that he had another tutor for Ginny who had been a specialist in remedial reading. Maybe she would be able to find the solution to Ginny's reading difficulties.

When the new tutor arrived, we had a brief conversation about the rest of the family. Roberta was upstairs in her crib at the time, but I mentioned the baby was a Mongoloid. Her first comment was, "How bad does she look?"

She questioned me about Ginny's capabilities. Something prompted me to quote Mr. Hrubes' earlier remark that she was ill —not handicapped. She watched Ginny coming into the room and asked me, "What do you mean, she's not handicapped. She walks just like a palsied child!"

Whenever this tutor finished a session, she quietly let herself out the front door, without any comment on her progress. If I wanted a report, I had to watch the clock and be there the exact second that the hour was over. She would answer my questions as briefly as possible, but several times made it quite clear that I was keeping her from more important things.

My earliest impressions had been unfavorable and kept getting worse. I spoke to Dan about it. He is the most charitable man I have ever known. When I gave my reports, he would warn me not to judge too quickly. She might be an excellent teacher; possibly she could overcome the reading problem. Maybe it would be good for Ginny to work with someone who obviously was not impressed by her accomplishments.

I kept reminding myself that Dan was right and I shouldn't let my evaluation of her teaching ability get confused with my personal feelings. But, she just did not seem to *like* Ginny.

Often, I was busy in the kitchen while the tutor worked with Ginny in the adjoining living room. Sometimes comments were loud and firm and carried above the rattling of dishes. It always seemed that she saw only faults and never acknowledged improvement. I had the feeling she was the proverbial person who could look at the most exquisite rose and her sole comment would be "such ugly thorns."

The weeks progressed faster than the work and, try as I would, I couldn't change my opinion. Ginny, possibly more than any other child, thrived on praise. She would do anything and endure everything, simply out of love.

The tutor certainly did not love her. I never heard her praise her. She was always stressing what was wrong. If the answers were correct, the comment was that the handwriting was unsteady, or too slow. If she read words correctly, her inflection was wrong.

This woman just never accepted the love that Ginny so freely exchanged with all the others who had worked with her.

Since we were not directly paying for her services, we felt we had no right to complain—not yet anyway. Possibly things would improve, given more time. Ginny always managed to derive a benefit from an obstacle, we told ourselves. We decided not to make an issue either with the tutor or with the school authorities, and in fact we stuck to that resolution for a considerable time.

Dr. Rosenzweig saw Ginny every few months to check on her progress. In mid-February he decided it was again time to have her kidney problem evaluated. He felt that she had reached a point where she could withstand surgery. He also knew our financial status. He contacted the urologist and asked him if he would do the job and cut his fee to the limit of our insurance, and not ask us to make up the difference. The urologist felt he could not do that. Dr. Rosenzweig told him he just wanted to be sure to have offered him the first chance to perform the operation. (Dr. Rosenzweig seemed to take the attitude that it was a privilege to work with Ginny; whether or not you got your full fee was secondary.) He called another urologist and again explained the financial problem. He came back to me, told what he had done. He had complete confidence in the surgical skill of both doctors, but since the second was willing to help us financially, he felt it wiser to change.

The following evening, the new urologist examined her. He showed me the X rays of her kidneys. When I first looked at them, all I could see was ribs. Then he explained what I was looking at, and it became obvious how enlarged the left kidney was. He said he could not promise anything. Until he operated, he could not make a decision if the kidney could be saved. He wanted to warn me of the real possibility that she might lose it. He felt, however, that on the evidence in the X rays, there was a chance it could be saved.

Not having any medical education, I could not fully understand exactly what he was going to do, but it seemed he would open up the constriction, and build a funnel-like link between the kidney and the tube. Again he warned me that because the constriction was at the junction of the kidney and the tube, it would be difficult and he couldn't make any promises.

Within a few days, the operation was scheduled. Two days before she was to leave, she was at the supper table with all the family and asked the other children, "When I'm in the hospital, will you kids all pray for me so it doesn't hurt much and I don't cry?"

All too quickly the day came, and we left for the hospital. She was frightened but put on a stanch front. She had to be catheterized and was openly afraid, having had a painful experience many months earlier. Diane, the nurse in pediatrics who was so close to Ginny, had the reputation for being most proficient at the job. She took Ginny to the treatment room, and a few minutes later came out all misty-eyed. She came over to me. "Do you know what she did? She 'offered it up' for all the other sick kids in the hospital."

When we visited in the evening, she was having a ball. Many of the staff had taken care of her at the time of the accident, and were delighted with her recovery. They gave her all freedom possible. She was busy serving soda to children who weren't allowed out of bed, having great fun and in good spirits. Earlier she had some apprehension about staying at the hospital again. But, this evening, not being in any discomfort, and allowed to get soda from the kitchen, she was completely satisfied with the idea of "sleeping over" for two weeks.

Because several tests had to be made, she was in the hospital for the whole weekend before any surgery was done. By Sunday evening, she was again a little apprehensive (but I'm sure not nearly so much as I).

The operation was scheduled for eight o'clock Monday morning. The doctor promised he would call as soon as it was over. I tried to keep busy, but was listening for the phone from 8:02 on. I kept trying to convince myself that the longer it took, the greater the possibility the kidney could be saved. I had decided if he removed the kidney it would take less time than if he was able to repair it. At that point, it did not matter if my supposition was correct medically, it gave me more patience. As long as the phone did not ring, her chances, in my own mind, were better.

As always when waiting, time seemed interminable, but finally the phone rang. The operation had gone well. He had not removed the kidney, but once again there was no simple "everything is going to be all right." So much still depended on how it healed, and how well it would function.

When I saw her, she was still under the effect of anesthesia. I sat by her bed and held her free hand. While the apparatus was simple, the intravenous bottle hanging above her bed, the needle in her arm, the sweet smell of the anesthesia still clinging to her breath, the limpness of her hand . . . brought back memories. She opened her eyes and in a weak little voice said, "Your hair looks *very* pretty, Mommy. And thank you for coming."

No complaints. No self-pity. I had to fight back the tears.

When the schedule of nurses was made for that day, Diane had asked if she could have Ginny. She had been so close to her at the time of recovery from the accident, she wanted to care for her on the day of this operation.

Ginny was so patient, good, and appreciative of every little thing Diane did for her. Each time Diane made her more comfortable, no matter how slightly, Ginny always thanked her. Her voice was so weak and sounded wracked with pain; it was heartbreaking and frequently Diane would step out into the hall to wipe away the tears.

She had been given Demerol for the pain but it made her vomit terribly. The following day they tried five baby aspirin. She retained them, but, possibly because of the damage to her brain from the accident, they wanted to keep her to an absolute minimum of medication. Those five little aspirin were all she had to ease the pain of a ten-inch incision. With the same little voice, she would say, "It hurts very much, but I'm trying to be a good girl because you asked me to."

Every time she was so stoic, Diane would say, "This would be much easier on me if she would scream and complain. She's just so good, it's eating my heart out."

As Dan and I walked down the hall to visit her the next evening, we passed the room where Gin had spent the first two months after the accident. The same neurosurgeons who had taken care of Ginny were working over a very still little form. So much of the apparatus was the same, it sent a chill through both of us.

We learned that it was a four-year-old girl, hit by a station wagon. She was in a coma, in much the same condition as Ginny had been.

We told Ginny about the other little girl; how she was hurt in a similar accident. Gin decided she would offer up her pain for the other girl. "God made me all better. He can make her all better."

We left a message with the nurses that if the parents wanted to talk to us, we were there. Dan felt it was better we did not approach them, but wait until they wanted to talk.

The following evening, the parents introduced themselves. It did them good to see Ginny recovering. As it had been with Ginny, the doctors could not promise them anything. Any hope for recovery they had to develop within themselves. Ginny gave them the hope they needed for their little girl.

To me, it seemed another example of God's goodness; Ginny was there at that particular time, to give them that hope. The possibility of the kidney operation had been open for over a year. Why was it precipitated so suddenly? Why did Ginny just happen to be there? It was the first serious accident victim they had had since Ginny. Maybe God knew that those parents would be helped by seeing her.

Ginny was in a great deal of pain, making it most difficult for her to move. The incision ran just above her waistline, starting under her ribs in the back and finishing under her ribs in front. Other than her right arm, there was little she could move without pulling the stitches. She was again on a catheter, and there was also a drain in the incision. There was no way she could get comfortable.

We tried to think of something to help entertain her. Dan had an idea and she was pleased with the solution. The following day he borrowed his brother's tape recorder. Each evening we took a message from every one of the children. Even Roberta did some "talking" at the insistence of the older children. It took much coaxing. She would just stare at the microphone, but she finally did gurgle and coo.

Ginny would listen to the whole tape and send back answers to each one, not forgetting, "Roberta, you be a good baby."

Each night the children would all wait up for us to come home. They had to know how Ginny was doing. They could check her progress each day by the tone of her voice. On one of the first tapes, to "How are you feeling?" she responded in a strained little voice, "Not very good. It hurts *very* much." In a few days, the voice was cockier, "John, send me a present like you said!"

Again, Ginny made friends, and had the other children in the room sending messages back and forth.

In spite of the intense pain, she still had her sense of independence and determination. The first time out of bed, she let two nurses help her walk because they insisted. She really would rather have tried it by herself. Two days after the operation, she did a sit-up in bed "to practice for therapy." That stunt was quickly stopped, for fear she would tear something open. But Diane had to "absolutely forbid" her to try it again, until she had permission from the doctor.

With strenuous exercise forbidden, and walking allowed only when accompanied by a nurse, her activities were limited to what she could do sitting in bed. Since she wasn't allowed out, she encouraged the other children in the ward to come in.

A little boy across the hall brought his paint set over to Gin's room to amuse her. Perched on the foot of her bed, he spread all his supplies between them. But the paper ran out too quickly. He went looking for more.

Sitting Indian-fashion, Ginny just started painting the most available spot . . . her toenails. And soon got carried away.

Diane came into the room for a routine check, and did a double take. *"Ginny, what are you doing?"*

Gin had painted her feet blue!

"If you're well enough to paint them, you're well enough to scrub them! I'm getting a basin of hot water and soap, and you're going to clean every bit of that paint off your feet right this minute!"

When we arrived at visiting hours, Diane met us in the hall to explain how the blue paint got under Ginny's toenails. "I've seen some odd things, but it's the first time I've ever had a kid with painted feet. All the time I was scolding her, I had to keep from laughing. She looked so funny . . . all the hospital equipment, the white hospital gown . . . and blue feet. But she knew she shouldn't have been doing it, and was just being an imp!"

When we came into Gin's room, she guiltily showed us her feet, and explained simply, "I wanted to paint but we didn't have any more paper, so I painted my feet!"

I was late for visiting hours one day. A new patient in the room was still under the effect of anesthesia. While waiting for him to wake up, his mother started talking to Ginny. They had only gotten into general conversation, so the woman knew nothing of Gin's accident. When I arrived, she remarked that she had never heard a child with such excellent diction! She found it hard to believe that there had been no speech a year earlier. I was elated because someone with complete impartiality had been honestly impressed.

Ten days after the operation they tested to see if the drain could be removed from the kidney. Blue dye was injected into the kidney through the tube, then the tube was clamped. If the urine was bright blue, the kidney was functioning. The first time on the bed-pan, she was enthusiastic about the color. To anyone who came into the room, she would proudly announce, "I can go *blue!*"

It was necessary to check every hour. I put her on the bedpan, took the specimen, and reported to the nurses. After several times, she caught on to the routine and giggled, "Tell Diane it's purple with pink polka dots."

It was functioning satisfactorily. The drain was removed. Every-thing seemed fine. The following night her bathrobe was soaked through. Something was forcing the urine to back up and seep through the unhealed opening in her side. It should have closed in one day. By Friday, it was three days, and it was still draining. It could have been just swelling that was causing it, or it could be scar tissue forming. The doctor was willing to give her till Monday, but he was concerned. He scheduled the operating room for Monday to do a cystoscope, a deep internal examination, requiring anesthesia.

When Diane heard the news, she was annoyed, "Why does every-thing have to happen to that kid. There are so many bratty, obnox-ious ones where nothing ever goes wrong. She's so good. Doesn't anything ever go easily for her?"

The unit clerk overheard her. She related to Diane what Dan had commented the previous night when he was told about Ginny's setback. "Things have been going too well for us. We were due for some problems."

The two of them exchanged a glance of admiration and disbelief. As she walked away, Diane asked herself out loud, "Why does it always happen to such nice people?"

We decided it was best not to tell Ginny ahead of time. She would worry too much and there was a whole weekend during which she would have it on her mind. It seemed better to let her rest and tell her just before it was time for the operation, on Mon-day morning.

The other little accident victim was still in the coma and had been on intravenous feedings. She had reached that point where it was felt she might be in the coma for an extended period. The in-travenous could not be continued indefinitely. As had been with Ginny's recovery from her accident, they would do a gastrostomy, inserting a feeding tube through the abdominal wall, directly into her stomach. She, too, was scheduled for Monday morning.

I went home to the other children and asked them to pray for two miracles in two days. They knew about the other little girl and had been praying for her all along. Now we were asking that she would regain enough consciousness to be able to eat; that Ginny's side would stop draining; and two operations would be avoided. The children were deeply concerned about both girls and went on an all-out campaign of "offering up" and "making sacrifices."

Saturday—everything was the same.

Sunday afternoon—everything was the same.

Sunday evening—Ginny's side stopped draining. Her operation was canceled!

We went home full of joy. We had one answer—one more to go. The relief concerning Ginny switched our total thoughts to the other girl's need.

Monday morning—she was taken to the operating room. As they prepared her for the surgery, she showed some signs of consciousness and someone tried to give her a sip of water. She swallowed it. The operation was canceled!

All of us were delighted. It fortified all the children's beliefs in the power of their prayers.

Ginny was watched carefully. When her kidney operation was first planned, the doctor had expected about fourteen days in the hospital. Ginny had overheard him. As we started the eighteenth day, she was getting very impatient. But, she wasn't the only one. John was upset about the duration of her stay. His anxiety was explained when he complained, "She missed my birthday last year. She better be home in time this year." Two years earlier, John couldn't stand Ginny. Now he wondered about the possibility of postponing his birthday until she came home.

She was discharged on the twentieth day, in time for the birthday. To her it seemed longer than the five months after the accident.

Once the other little girl was able to take food orally, she progressed rapidly and, within a few weeks, was discharged. When I told Ginny the news, for the first and only time during her illness she said something that resembled self-pity. "How come she got better so fast, and it took me so long?"

I explained that her own head must have been hurt more (and inwardly I knew that many of the things they had learned with Ginny, new treatments that were tried and proved effective, had helped the other girl's recovery).

Gin never questioned it again.

***

CHAPTER 27

MARCH 16, 1968 WOULD BE THE FIRST ANNIVERSARY OF GINNY'S HOME-coming. We wanted to do something especially appropriate to mark the occasion.

At that time, permission had just been granted in our diocese for "home Masses," dependent on approval by the local pastor. Monsignor had been pastor of our parish for only a year, and as yet I did not know him well. I had no idea how he regarded "home Masses" but did know that he was cautious about encouraging some of the recent innovations. If we could, we wanted to have a Mass at home to celebrate the occasion.

There were many possibilities open—if we could get permission. We could ask the priest who had anointed her; it would be appropriate for him to say the Mass. That might not be possible, because it would be a Saturday evening, and he might have to hear confessions. The next best chance was Dan's brother, who was a Capuchin priest. If we couldn't have one, maybe we could have the other. But I still needed the initial okay from Monsignor.

By the time I got to the rectory door, I had gone over my whole plea so often I was positive I would not be given permission—under any circumstances.

Monsignor greeted me most warmly and cordially. He knew about Ginny and inquired about her progress. It gave me an opening to start my speech.

I explained about the anniversary, and the desire to have a home Mass. I wondered if it would be possible to have the priest who had answered her sick call, because of his involvement with her recovery.

Monsignor was sorry, but he really needed Father for Saturday confessions.

I immediately tried my second line of defense. I was sure that Dan's brother would be available that evening (since he was attending college for his master's degree and was free on the weekends), if we had permission.

Monsignor thought a minute. I could feel him searching for the words to tell me gently, but firmly, that he didn't approve of home Masses.

When he finally started, I was stricken. He began, "I don't want to upset anything within the family. If you would prefer Dan's brother, that is your choice. But, I would really like to come and say the Mass myself."

I had built up the whole question to a point that I was sure it just would not be allowed. I had never even considered the possibility that I should have asked him first. I said I really did not think it was reasonable to add to his great responsibilities and hoped I had not offended him by not asking for him first.

I was immensely pleased; I couldn't thank him enough.

By the time I got home, I was going over a mental list of all who should be included. The living room was large; we could easily include everyone who had a part in Ginny's recovery—and their children. Our parents, brothers and sisters, all the baby sitters, the nurses and the many friends who had helped us; a quick count totaled almost a hundred and fifty. The living room wasn't *that* large. As much as I had wanted to include them, I started by eliminating all children except ours. By the time I finished with phone calls, between sixty and seventy were coming.

As more and more arrived that evening, the older children had doubts about the room being large enough. I reminded them, "If Christ fed all those people out of one basket of fish, He can get sixty-five in our living room." There was a little overflow into the front hall, but everyone who could be, was there.

It was beautiful. I had never before been that close to a Mass, never before felt so much a part of it.

Monsignor read the Mass of the day. The epistle was of Jacob, Isaac and Esau and the greatest blessing not always going to the first born. The gospel was of the prodigal son and the great rejoicing over the child "thought dead" having returned.

Dan wrote a "Prayer of the Faithful":

> *That the priests and religious who comforted Virginia's family during the long months of her coma always continue to teach others to have faith in their darkest hours, we pray to you O Lord:*
>
> *Lord, hear our prayer.*
>
> *That the doctors, nurses and medical technicians who aided Virginia in her recovery always continue to have hope for even the most hopeless of patients in their care, we pray to you O Lord:*
>
> *Lord, hear our prayer.*
>
> *That the friends and neighbors who volunteered their help to Virginia's family in so many ways during her convalescence always continue to demonstrate their charity for others, we pray to you O Lord:*
>
> *Lord, hear our prayer.*
>
> *Accept the thanks of all here present, O Lord, for Your mercy in sparing the life of this child. And, permit us the joy of seeing her develop in wisdom and maturity. Through Jesus Christ, Your Son, Our Lord, who lives and reigns with You in the unity of the Holy Spirit, God, forever and ever. Amen.*

All through the months Ginny was so sick, the Communion prayer had impressed me deeply, particularly the last half ". . . speak but the word and my soul will be healed." I firmly believed that God simply had to "say the word" and my "soul" would be healed.

But now the first half of the prayer was equally meaningful. Gathered here were all our family and friends, giving thanks to God for having granted us the privilege to be part of a wondrous miracle. Now the prayer started, "Lord, I am not worthy that you should come under my roof . . ."

So often before these people had been here to take care of the children, help with housework, and earlier to offer sympathy. Now we were gathered, united in deepest gratitude and joy.

✱✱✱

CHAPTER 28

Ginny was determined that she was going to "get all better." She was always vibrantly enthusiastic when she relearned something she had done well before the accident. Our eighty-year-old house had a big open stairwell. She spent all spring trying to slide down the banister, under her father's supervision. The first trips were slow and shaky, with Dan supporting her all the way for balance.

After much practice, she could go up the stairs, climb on the banister and slide down while Dan watched from below. Standing in the lower hall, I prayed that she would not fall off.

They continued to work at it, but I wasn't aware that they were doing anything more than exercising an accomplishment. Generally they would practice in the evening. I was busy in the kitchen at that time preparing dinner.

After one special session, she came to me giddy with excitement. "I can slide down the banister—*no hands!* Want to see?"

It took a lot of nerve but she did it. Dan watched proudly; my heart was in my throat.

As the weather became warm, she went out to play with the other children more frequently. Many times the games were more than she could handle; she would reorganize the group into something she could play on equal terms. The children in the neighborhood all shared in her improvement, and were willing to play her games, constantly coaxing her to greater strides, without taking advantage of her limitations.

One of Alice's daughters appointed herself as Ginny's teaching aide. Each day she'd come and struggle to alleviate the reading difficulty. It seemed Ginny just needed much practice. On balmy days they'd go outside and settle under a tree to study. I'd look out the window and see them laboring word by word, her "teacher's" arm encircling Gin's shoulder, lending physical as well as moral support.

But Bernadette was still closest to Ginny. She still had a lot of natural common sense, patience and goodness. She worked and coached, helping Gin to ride her bike (with training wheels) and climb trees (if only to the first limb).

The two of them came flying into the house one afternoon—Dettie was flying and Ginny was making every effort at a close second. They were out of breath with excitement. Dettie was bubbling, "Mommy! Ginny can jump rope! Really! I taught her. Come on, we'll show you!"

We all trooped out to the driveway. Celia took one end of the rope, Dettie the other. Ginny would get all set. They would turn slowly, and Dettie would cue her, "Now jump!" It took several tries, but she finally cleared it.

There was much pride and congratulations all around.

Her confidence built up and the inevitable happened. She fell. Dettie ran to her, helped her up and, with deep understanding, consoled her, "That's okay. I fall sometimes, too. But let's practice over on the lawn so it doesn't hurt when you fall."

Pride was restored, confidence regained—and the game went on.

In the previous September, when I looked forward to a full year of tutoring, I had hoped that Ginny would be able to accomplish the work of two years in one. As we were beginning May, I had some question as to whether we would even get through the first-grade work.

Tutoring was a constant chore. For a most profitable one-to-one relationship, mutual love should have developed. I had hoped my early evaluation of this tutor was wrong, that a rapport would grow. But it never did. The tutor just seemed to be unable to show any warmth toward Ginny. She felt that we had overprotected her and spoiled her; that the children did too much for her. To this I responded that I honestly felt the children did for Ginny what I would want them to do for any person—"give all the help you are able, wherever it is needed." As to the charge that we had spoiled her, I did not agree but it is difficult for a mother to evaluate this herself.

The tutor seemed as unhappy with the situation as I. The table Ginny used for a desk was too shaky. I found a steadier one. That was too low. It was impossible for the tutor to gain absolute concentration if there was any distraction from the other children. (Miss Engel once told me if children could learn to work with distraction around them, it would be invaluable. One seldom has the opportunity to work in complete isolation.) This tutor used to scold Ginny for not paying attention; not watching what she was working on. (She always sat at Ginny's left side, and it was Gin's left eye that drifted uncontrollably.)

I became more and more unhappy with the situation, but felt that I still had no right to complain since the school system was supplying the tutor. Then I suddenly realized that if the school was also paying for the tutor, and the work was not progressing because of an unfavorable relationship, my not complaining was costing the school system money.

Still reluctant to make a complaint to the school, I was uneasy as I called Mr. Hrubes. As objectively as I could, I explained the situation. He was most understanding and agreed that there are cases where a pupil and tutor do not work well together. When he had first sent her, he had thought it would be profitable. We had given it ample time; obviously it wasn't working out.

He wondered, also, about plans for the following September. He suggested, if agreeable to us, we have Ginny tested—intellectually and psychologically. Never having met her himself, he asked if he could stop at the house one day to add his own evaluation to the tests that would be made.

When he arrived, Ginny was still upstairs getting dressed. He noticed Roberta in her playpen. I'm sure from his experience, he knew she was a Mongoloid, but waited for me to tell him. We had quite a lengthy conversation regarding the baby. He gave me reassurance that we were doing the right things for her: simply accepting her and loving her as any other child, giving her what help she needed and expecting her to do all she was capable of.

He had warmth and understanding that Ginny responded to immediately. In the course of the "interview" he was sitting on the floor with her, playing cards. He apologized to her for not knowing the game. Would she teach him? By his deliberately "not knowing how to play" he learned more about her mental and physical ability than if he had tried a dozen formal tests. Her ability (or attempt) to shuffle and deal, her speech, her communication were all obvious to him.

He felt it would be profitable to go ahead with the formal tests and arranged an appointment. She was excited about visiting "real school" again.

The woman who administered the tests knew nothing of Ginny's history. After a prolonged session, she came out to interview me, while Ginny worked alone on a timed exam. "Is it true that Ginny was hit by a truck on October 25, 1966?" When I nodded, she said, "Well, that's what she told me, and it sounded as if she knew what she was talking about."

She was impressed by Ginny's industry, her desire to please. She would stop during the work and ask, "Am I doing this right?" "Is this the way you want it done?"

The tests lasted for two and a half hours. They would still have to be scored and evaluated but the psychologist felt that Ginny had no "hang-ups" regarding the accident.

Until the tests were marked, and some decision reached, we were to continue with the same tutor. Because it was already the middle of May, it seemed probable that we would have her until the end of the term. I was determined to make an all-out effort to learn to like her. The more I tried, though, the more I realized that we lived in two different worlds. Our feelings on what was important in life were miles apart.

I thought that I was making a little progress in my campaign until she related an incident. Her brother came to visit her in her brand-new home. He brought a friend who was crippled and had braces on his legs. She was afraid that he would scratch her new furniture.

My attempts at understanding her were shattered. I told the story to Dan. He asked me not to be too quick to judge. "Maybe she felt it would embarrass him if the furniture was scratched."

He was much kinder than I. From what I had learned of her, the only things that mattered were her clothes, her house, and whether or not she was out of our home in time to play tennis, while a "woman who comes in" took care of her children.

Ginny's work did seem to be improving slightly, but rather than the hour of tutoring, I think it was the hours every day that I had to spend helping her do her homework. That tutor had even given Ginny homework the last day before her kidney operation, "so she would have something to do." To this, Dan's reaction was that she may have felt it would take Ginny's mind off the impending surgery.

At last, results of the tests were evaluated. Mr. Hrubes felt Ginny would do better in a classroom situation. Even though he had earlier hoped she would return to regular classes, it seemed she was not quite ready for it. There were two possibilities open; "special classes" in the public elementary school or a school for the handicapped in our county.

I was disappointed. Deep down, all through that year and a half, I had hoped she would recover well enough to go back with the other children. But, I had to be honest with myself—for her own good. She was not walking well enough to be able to handle herself at dismissal time with a surging mob of children. Her schoolwork was nowhere near a level convenient for regular classes. Her reading and spelling were only halfway through first grade. Her math scored halfway through second grade, even though she had been "taught" only part of the first-grade work.

Mr. Hrubes wanted us to observe classes at both schools to help in making the decision.

When we visited the school for the handicapped, we were impressed. I had never been in a public institution where there was such a genuine air of warmth—teachers, pupils and employees all radiated it. Everyone was handicapped, some most severely. But it seemed that people who had big problems of their own were more ready to understand others.

They interviewed Ginny while we filled out forms, pages and pages of forms. The one that stumped us was the question, "Marital status of parents." Dan looked at me, "What do we put down, 'happy'?"

It did seem the school offered a facility for children much more severely afflicted than Ginny. Another result of the visit was a recognition that it was a long trip every day. Even though bus service would be provided, over an hour each day would be devoted to traveling. The school doctor who had examined Ginny agreed the distance was a disadvantage and joked that the only thing the children learn on the bus is how to throw spitballs.

Soon afterward, we had the opportunity to visit the "special class" in our own public school. It was a non-graded first-to-third group. Maximum capacity was fifteen students. They worked in small groups, individually if necessary. When a student's ability warranted it, he attended regular classes in the school. The group was a mixture of many problems, including another child recovering from an accident, and a Mongoloid.

The most impressive part of the whole class was the teacher, Mrs. Cereste. A tall, blond woman, she carried herself with a poise that comes from confidence bred by success. She had the wisdom of many years in special education, and the vigor of youth; a smile that could win the trust of the most timid, and a glare that could tame the truant. She obviously loved those children without any slushiness, accepted them without pity, and understood them.

We were sure this was the place for Ginny. The next question would be whether Mrs. Cereste and Mr. Hrubes felt Ginny was right for the class.

Another wait—another interview. Mr. Hrubes went over her records with me. Ginny's I.Q. tested at only 77, but he quickly qualified that. He explained that everyone who had worked with her felt this was harshly low and due primarily to the still-existing vision problem from injury to her left-eye muscles. Because she wrote slowly, she did not score well on timed tests. Because she had difficulty keeping her vision aligned, it was almost impossible for her to find the correct box to mark, even if she knew the answer.

He felt she would do well in Mrs. Cereste's class. Even though I had earlier hoped for regular school, by now I was well satisfied and pleased with his decision.

In the course of establishing a file on Ginny, he had gathered information from many of the doctors who had worked with her. I had gotten permission from the doctors to go over those records; every one mentioned her good spirits and sense of humor.

The most interesting was the progression of reports from the neurosurgeons. After all the technical, clinical information, each report was summarized with a general evaluation.

They read:

The day of the accident—"The outcome of this case does not appear very favorable."

Discharge from the hospital—"She is showing improvement."

Four months later—"Continued improvement."

One year after the accident—"Changes have been *most* remarkable."

Recalling the chronic terse pessimism the neurosurgeons had always shown during those days, that report was vibrant with enthusiasm!

It was all settled. She would go to school in September. The bus would pick her up the day after Labor Day. She would start with a half-day schedule because she still fatigued readily. She would be given extra time to complete her work because of her vision problems.

In my heart I could make one prediction. Based on Mrs. Cereste's ability, and Ginny's compatibility, she would do well.

Every time Ginny saw a little yellow bus pass our house, she asked, "When summer's over, is that the bus that will take me to school?"

* * *

CHAPTER 29

THE DECISION ABOUT GINNY'S SCHOOLING WAS SETTLED, BUT THERE were still other questions. The muscle imbalance in her eyes was being watched. Her control of the left eye was improving and they were apparently focusing together more frequently. The ophthalmologist checked her eyes regularly, but felt he had to wait at least two years after the accident before he could recommend any correction. He knew such a severe blow would take at least two years to heal. He would not risk doing any corrective surgery only to have it undone, possibly in the opposite direction, by continued natural healing. So that question still hung in the back of my mind.

Then there was the matter of her kidney. The urologist wanted her brought back three months after the surgery, for X rays. She had been doing so well . . . no fever, no pain, none of the problems that were considered "trouble signs." I took her for the X rays expecting that everything would be fine and something would finally be finished . . . completely cured.

Ginny questioned why the tests had to be made. I explained the doctor could see how the outside was healing; this would tell him how the inside was healing. She thought a minute, then added, "He wants to see if he did a good job. And if it's all messy, he'll have to operate on me again."

Her matter-of-factness threw me. I hadn't even considered that possibility. She was doing so well, I had complete confidence. *This* was going to be all right.

Dye was injected into her arm; this would travel into the kidneys and show patterns on the X ray. She was afraid; but she was very brave. And as things often went with her, her veins were difficult to penetrate and they had to try twice till they succeeded. The doctor, although most proficient, seemed annoyed with himself because it had been painful for Gin. He asked the question I had heard voiced often before, "Why are things always so difficult for *her?*"

Afterward she asked me, "Know why I didn't cry? I wanted to be a big girl." Then admitted, "But I was scared."

She lay on her back, without moving, for two hours. About every fifteen minutes an X ray was taken, then developed, then examined by the doctor. This continued until he had the information he wanted.

Finally it was finished and I went to see him in his office for his report. I was still riding high, confident that at last this phase of her recovery was going to be completed.

His voice was grave . . . the X rays showed an obstruction. He explained that it could be swelling or it could be scar tissue forming. While he was talking, Ginny's earlier statement kept running through my mind, ". . . And if it's all messy, he'll have to operate on me again."

"Dear God, please. Don't let it be more surgery for her."

The doctor decided to wait six months, then do more X rays. If it was simply swelling, it would be healed by then. If it was scar tissue . . . He didn't have to elaborate.

It had been a long hard siege. In spite of the disappointing report from the urologist and some unanswered questions, things were beginning to look promising.

All these long months my mother had been caring for my brother's children. Now, Joe had met a wonderful girl. She had lost her husband in an accident when her two children were quite young. They had set the date to be married.

When Joe told his children, they were delighted. One of his daughters confided in my mother, "I'm so glad. She's great, and I can talk to her about anything."

Roberta was coming along beautifully. I took her back to the neurologist. He was pleased with her. It was the first good "doctor's report" that we had had in a long time. She was about twenty-one months and able to pull herself to her feet, and "walk" around her playpen, as long as she was holding the side. She was beginning to eat table food. She could blow her nose! All in all, she was a little angel. And at that point, I really didn't care when she learned to walk and talk.

Ginny was going on eight. I had hoped she would make her first Communion at the anniversary Mass we had at home. Monsignor felt it might be too much excitement. Now I began to think she would really rather make it at church with the rest of her class as her two older sisters had done.

I called the Sister who had charge of the first-Communion class. She had been following Ginny's progress and was pleased that she would be able to receive Communion with the rest of the children. She would make whatever arrangements were necessary. A place would be saved in the first row. Dan could just bring her in and get her settled in the pew. She wouldn't have to make the long procession on the slick terrazzo floor.

There was some concern as to whether or not she knew enough of the religion to receive. When I told her she could make her Communion, she asked, "You mean I can take 'the pill'?" They were wondering if she knew enough for first Communion! It sounded as though she should have been in a pre-Cana conference.

As far as her knowledge of religion was concerned, she had little formal training. But she certainly understood, better than most eight-year-olds, her dependence on God and her relationship to other people.

When she went to the Communion practice, she was excited as well as apprehensive. Because she wasn't to be in the procession, we waited in the church, while the other children lined up. She asked about many things, then questioned me about the confessional. It had been decided that she would not make her confession at that time. Although she had been through much, giving her a deep grasp of many spiritual concepts, still she was too young to interpret the meaning of confession. But, she did have some knowledge of what it meant from conversations with the older children. I told her that in a few years she could go to confession. She agreed, "When I'm older, and I can understand."

Preparations were under way. Since Alice was her godmother, she wanted to make a new dress for her. But, her oldest daughter, just a few years earlier, had worn a most beautiful dress. It was so sweet and simple, and fitted Ginny perfectly, in size and personality. If Alice did not mind, I hoped Ginny would wear that dress.

She needed new shoes, and I had spoken to the Sister in charge of the class about it. Gin really had to have a good pair of everyday oxfords. Most conventional "Communion" shoes have soles slippery as ice; I was concerned about her safety while walking. Sister agreed it would be better all around to get her the oxfords, as there would be less risk of her falling.

Since many of the children needed shoes at the time, we made a mass excursion to the shoe store.

We decided on a practical red oxford. Ginny had been telling the salesman about her first Communion. He asked if I wanted white shoes for her. I explained why she needed special support, and my fear of the slick soles on the stone floor in church. He disappeared into the back of the shop and found a pair of little white pumps . . . with roughened soles. He fitted them, then put them back in the box and handed it to her. "That's a present from me."

Then he leaned over to me. "Every little girl should have white shoes for her Communion."

Even though the morning was cool and overcast, it seemed a glorious day. When she was all dressed, she was radiant; it was hard to decide if she looked more like a princess or an angel.

The whole procession was filing into their rows. Dan helped Ginny across the front aisle to her place in the first pew. We stood by the side . . . and watched . . . and prayed . . . and remembered.

In the whole twenty-month period, I had never been so completely overcome. My heart was brimful with complete unbridled joy. It kept spilling over into tears streaming down my face. The harder I tried to contain them, the more freely they flowed. We had been granted a miracle.

My mind kept flashing back. That afternoon in the emergency room. The doctor's voice, "She has a one-in-a-million chance to make it through the night." Now here she was, so fully aware of God's love for her.

Twenty-six years ago, to the day, I had knelt there to make my own first Communion. I had been so innocent of the things life was to hold for me.

Again my mind drifted back to the emergency room. Ginny had

received the last rites to prepare her for heaven. Now she would receive our Lord to strengthen her for life.

The necessity to do the tracheotomy. The day that her lung collapsed. The months, the soul-searing months with no speech. Now her voice carried all the way into the sanctuary.

The children stood to go to the altar rail. Ginny was standing with them. That little girl who had suffered so . . . who had been so hopeless . . . was all fulfillment.

Monsignor's voice was steady, "The Body of Christ."

Ginny's was clear, "Amen."

So be it!

✸✸✸

POSTSCRIPT

THE FOLLOWING FALL, ALMOST TWO YEARS AFTER THE ACCIDENT, GINNY returned to school, to Mrs. Cereste's class. Because a full day was considered too long for her, I was to bring her home at lunchtime. Arriving a few minutes early, I waited at the principal's office for her dismissal. I was never more anxious over a "first day at school," not even when any one of the children started kindergarten.

Finally, the bell rang. On Mrs. Cereste's arm, Gin arrived at the office . . . in tears. I couldn't imagine what went wrong. *Nothing* had gone wrong; the problem was simply that she wanted no part of the half-day routine. "All the other kids are staying. Why can't I stay?"

The principal commented, "In all the years I've been in schools, they've cried for a lot of reasons—but never because the day ended too soon. This is the only time I ever had a child cry because she had to go *home!*"

The following day, the schedule was adjusted. Ginny went the full day, as long as we brought her home for lunch. It gave her a quiet hour to rest, and was a little safer than "free play" in the schoolyard.

Our expectations of Mrs. Cereste had been an underestimate. She accomplished wonders. Gin's reading improved greatly although it remained below her grade level. Not only did she make academic progress, but she also reached physical feats that I would not have guessed possible.

Mrs. Cereste kept coaxing and coaching till finally she had Gin standing on a balancing board only ten inches wide, a foot above the floor, rocking back and forth in mid-air.

Ginny had homework, assignments, field trips and tests (and was heartbroken if there was anything less than 100 per cent). She even was part of the chorus in the school play. She belonged.

By the end of that year, she was taking her lunch, playing with the children in the schoolyard, and enjoying the full day. She received extra help with her speech and reading; attended music, art, library and *gym* with the regular second grade.

The kidney problem has not been completely cured. Each year she is X-rayed. Each time it shows some obstruction. While the kidney will never be "normal," it is functioning in a limited way, and the sequence of X rays indicates that it will not get worse.

Her eyes have been examined each year. On the earlier tests, she was unable to control the muscles, particularly in her left eye. The doctor had been considering surgery but kept postponing it because she showed some healing. At her last examination we had good news; she has achieved an almost perfect vision. God is good.

After not seeing Gin for almost two years, Raleigh had an opportunity to visit, in the fall of 1969. Pleased with the vast improvement, she commented, "Ginny will have no trouble overcoming any residual problems. There is really nothing that she won't be able to do."

Her analysis agreed with that of the neurosurgeons. In May of 1969, two and a half years after the accident, they discharged Ginny from their care. Unless something unusual comes up, it won't be necessary for them to see her again. She still has limitations, but they felt confident that she will, in time, either overcome or learn how to compensate for them.

They were referring specifically to her walking. She still had a somewhat awkward gait, still stepped high to get over her dropped foot. This problem is serious. She has developed the habit of throwing the right toes out to the side and, in so doing, she is forcing her ankle out of alignment with the rest of the bones in her leg and foot.

To correct this she wears a lightweight brace, with a spring mechanism to lift the toes. At one point, in the early days of her recovery, braces and other aids had been discussed. Though I didn't mention my distaste, I didn't like the idea. Braces were for handicapped children. My Ginny was going to recover; she wouldn't need braces. Now, looking back, a brace on one leg seems a small matter.

The doctors had some concern that it might be difficult for her psychologically. They were right. When I told Ginny she would be getting the brace, she balked. "Some of the kids laugh at me 'cause I walk funny. If I wear a brace, they'll make more fun of me."

We talked it over. If the brace helped her to walk better, and would help her foot, it would be worth it. And I still had an ace in the hole. The girls in Ginny's school had permission to wear slacks in bad weather. But I had always been rigid on the matter. "You're a young lady; you go to school dressed like a young lady." On the bitter winter days, I would relent. But in general, no slacks for school.

Now with her concern about the appearance of the brace, I decided it was time for an amendment to the rule. There was no objection from the school; Ginny could wear slacks all the time. In September of 1970 she started wearing a light brace, just up to her knee on her right leg . . . neatly concealed by a brand-new pair of bell-bottoms.

It improved her walking, the slacks hid it completely, and she was less conspicuous than she had been when she walked with the limp.

The brace was attached to high shoes. As she pulled them out of the box, her face lit up. "Mommy, they're beautiful. They look just like the boots the big girls wear!"

So much for her ability to adjust! The popular fashion fads of high boots and bell-bottom pants had solved two problems.

Ginny has been promoted to a higher level, but is still in the special classes. Once, Mrs. Cereste had incorporated Gin's problems, most tactfully, into class lessons on safety. Another teacher asked Ginny to give a demonstration to the class; how the brace worked, what it was doing for her foot, and why other people sometimes wear braces.

Ginny had enough self-confidence to explain, "Some people's eyes need a little help—they wear glasses; some people's teeth need help—they wear braces on their teeth. My foot needs a little help—so I wear a brace on my leg." The class was fascinated, and I'm sure from that day forward had more respect for anyone who "needed a little help with anything."

As this is written, it is four and a half years since Ginny's accident. Her recovery has not been complete. In my more honest moments, I admit she is brain-injured and is handicapped . . . slightly.

She has difficulty with some of her studies and she still has some unsteadiness; some lack of co-ordination. She still attends the special class, receiving extra help when needed. She occasionally feels frustrated by her limitations, particularly in outdoor activities.

But, for a child who could not live for twenty-four hours at the time of the accident, her limitations seem slight. She cares for herself completely; feeding, bathing, dressing, walking . . . and even sometimes running. She is able to shampoo her own hair, and has almost mastered the knack of a straight part down the back of her head, to make her pigtails. And she can dive into water over her head . . . and swim.

Her speech is very good, almost normal; with her brace, her walking has improved substantially, close to reaching a smooth naturalness. She maintains her high spirits, warm personality and dogged determination. And she is maturing into a very pretty young lady.

Is she handicapped? Certainly she has some physical limitations, but she also has a zest for life and a love of God and fellowman that some never achieve. Who shall decide . . . handicapped or . . . privileged?

In her eleven years of life, through her inspiration and influence, she has left a little part of the world a bit better because she was there. How many of us can claim as much?

Ginny's gift given to all who have known her was summed up by her first "special teacher." When Gin was promoted, Mrs. Cereste wrote, "My heart feels a tender sadness that my job has been done. She is a beautiful person and I do indeed thank God for having known her."

* * *

ACKNOWLEDGMENTS

Besides my husband, Dan; his mother, Mrs. Virginia Carson; and my parents, Mr. and Mrs. Joseph Koelbel, Sr., my thanks go to many whose help made this story possible: Dr. Andrew Agaloff; Sister Agnes (Therese Kaiven); Maria Alexandrov; Jeanne Barbato; Jeanne, Ursula and Barney Berry; Joan and Ben Breitung; Cathy Brennan; Mr. and Mrs. Clement Burns; Mary Burns; Dr. Stephen D. Burstein; Beth Callahan; Mr. and Mrs. Charles Carson; Diane and Jim Carson; Father John Carson; Marie and Tom Carson; Terence Carson; Ann Cereste; Dolores and Brian Clancy; Mrs. Isabel Clancy; Pat Collins; Helen Colwell; Jane Coyne; Bill DeFraine; Mary Jane DeMott; Mr. and Mrs. Joe DiGennaro; Fran and Brian Donovan; Cathy and Connie Drew; Dr. Arthur B. Duel; Dr. Herbert L. Elias; Linda Engel; Diana Erickson; Irene Farley; Ed Faulkner; Ann Fisenne; Dr. Oliver French; Dr. Stephen R. Fromm; Father Charles A. Gartner; Mrs. Ann Garvey; Dr. Samuel M. Gelfand; Dr. Frank M. Green; Dr. I. Melbourne Greenberg; Richard M. Guilderson, Jr.; Monsignor Richard H. J. Hanley; Fran Hart; Pam Hayes; Ilsa Heinz; Joan Heiple; Betty Higgins; Dr. Milton Holtzman; Mr. Joseph Hrubes; Fran Iandiorio; Raleigh Johnston; Agnes and Fritz Koelbel; Marie and Bill Koelbel, Trudy and Joe Koelbel; Mr. and Mrs. William Koelbel; Dr. Harold A. Kozinn; Dr. Stanley J. Landau; Monsignor Joseph F. Lawlor; Dr. Bernard P. Leonard; Dr. Edwin R. Linwood; Pat and Tom Lundgren; Sister Madonna (Joan Grace); Mrs. Mathilde Marchand; Anne Maroney; Mrs. Walter Mensching; Dr. Frederick U. Metcalf; Mildred Miller; Mrs. Nelson; Dr. Salvatore L. Noto; Mr. and Mrs. Fred Ossman;

Diane Paquet; Mrs. Pepper; Mary Pulick; Peggy Raudies; Mrs. Yvonne Raven; Jane Reinert; Mrs. Hugo Ricca; Dr. Norman Ronis; Mrs. K. Rose; Dr. Leonard F. Rosenzweig; Mrs. Joseph Rowan; Peg Rowan; Sister St. James (Theresa Miller); Penny Saunders; Joanne Schienke; Mollie Schuback; Rita Silverstein; Jo Spano; Alice and Lee Steedle; Dr. J. P. Stivelman; Mr. and Mrs. John Thorpe; Virginia Torre; Mrs. Gerard Venter; Frank Volz; Eileen Ward; Ellen Warren; Eileen White; Mrs. Marion Williams.

There were many more. Some names I've inadvertently omitted; other names I never learned. Though they are not mentioned here, I'm sure they are recorded in a more important Book.

I thank them. And united with all these friends . . . I thank God.

***